Quaker Meeting: A Risky Business

by
Eric W. Johnson

DORRANCE PUBLISHING CO., INC.
643 SMITHFIELD STREET
PITTSBURGH, PENNSYLVANIA 15222

Copyright © 1991 by Eric W. Johnson
All Rights Reserved
ISBN # 0-8059-3197-X
Printed in the United States of America

Second Printing

Some of Eric Johnson's Other Books

Textbooks

Improve Your Own Spelling
Language for Daily Use (co-author)
How to Achieve Competence in English
Learning to Achieve: The Basic Basic (co-author)
    Three workbooks: grades 4-7; 6-9; 9-12
You Are the Editor
English Handbook: How to Read, Speak, and Write Well

Trade books

How to Live through Junior High School
How to Live with Parents and Teachers
Teaching School: Points Picked Up
Raising Children to Achieve: a Guide for Motivating Success in School and Life
Love and Sex in Plain Language
Love and Sex and Growing Up
Sex: Telling It Straight
People, Love, Sex, and Families
The Family Book about Sexuality (co-author)
An Introduction to Jesus of Nazareth: a Book of Information and a Harmony of the
    Gospels
Older and Wiser: Wit, Wisdom, and Spirited Advice from the Older Generation
A Treasury of Humor: an Indexed Collection of Anecdotes
Humorous Stories About the Human Condition
The Stolen Ruler
Escape into the Zoo

Table of Contents

Introduction: Quakers? Risky Business? 1
    A Caution 2
    Some Uses for This Book 3
    The Index 3

I.   Quaker Meetings, What Are They? 5
    A Straightforward Explanation 5
    Quaker Meetings, Many Meanings 6
    Quaker Meetings: Source of Energy—a Catholic View 7
    So Where Is the Riskiness? Some Samples 8
        Comical 9
        Outrageous 10
        Inspiring or Wise or Both 10

II. Some Outrageous Meeting Happenings 13

III. Some Insights; Messages about Children;
    Dramatic Experiences; the Nature of God, Christ, Jesus 21
    Insights 21
    Children 26
    Dramatic Experiences 28
    The Nature of God, Christ, Jesus 34

IV. The Force of Meetings; Famous Quakers; Noises from
    the Outside World; Inspiring Words and Thoughts 40
    The Wonderful Force of Meetings 40
    Speaking about Famous Quakers 42
    Noises from the Outside World Enter Meeting for Worship 43
    Some Inspiring, Thought-provoking Words Quoted
    or Said in Meetings 44
    Some Brief, Inspiring Themes 47

V. Comical and Humorous Messages 51

VI.	Children in Meeting — Something Special	60

    Children's Messages — Intentional and Unintentional 61
    Children's Reactions to Messages 62
    More Reactions for Meetings for Worship, Spiritual
       and Otherwise 63
    Some Children's Mischief and Troubles in Meeting 64
    Ways to Keep Children Out of Trouble in Meeting—
       Mostly Discovered by the Kids Themselves 65

VII. Meetings for Worship in Friends' Schools 67
    Meetings in Elementary School 69
    Meetings in Upper School 72
    Messages That Stimulated All Worshipers 73
    Memorable Bits in School Meetings 73
    Some Events During Meeting for Worship 74
    A Few Actual Meetings for Worship 76

VIII. Quaker Meetings for Business — Sometimes Risky 80
    Getting Organized 80
    Faith and Practice 80
    Sense of the Meeting 81
    Some Incidents in Meetings for Business —
       a Mix of Wonderful, Humorous, Outrageous 82

IX. Quaker Weddings and Memorial Services 86
    Quaker Weddings 86
       Variations 87
       Risks 89
    Quaker Memorial Services 90

X. Some "Gathered" Meetings for Worship 94
    Brief Examples, and Explanations 94
    More Gathered Meetings 97

XI. Conclusion: Always New Beginnings 105
    How Some People Come to Join Friends 105
    What About You? 106
    Contributors to This Book 107
    Index 108

Introduction: Quakers? Risky Business?

The title of this book may surprise most readers, even Quaker readers. Members of the Religious Society of Friends, known as "Quakers" because they used to "quake before the Lord," are generally thought of as a quiet, prudent, even cautious group. So how is it that their Quaker Meetings for Worship can be correctly called a risky business?

Not Like That Movie

First, let me assure you that it is not because they are like the 1983 movie *Risky Business*, a film featuring a prostitute (played by Rebecca DeMornay) and a wealthy 17-year-old adolescent (played by Tom Cruise). The film was a mediocre grouping of stereotypes. However the title is catchy and also true about Quaker meetings. That's why I use it.

So why are Quaker Meetings a risky business? It's not because they are in any way a comedy for teenagers about love, sex, and money. It's because many of them are "unprogrammed"—that is, Friends gather for silent worship, with no pastor or order of service, and anything can happen, and often does.

My Own Meeting Experience

I personally know that this is true, for I figure that, not even counting about thirty Meetings at which I was present *in utero*, I've attended slightly over five thousand Meetings for Worship thus far in my life and am still going strong. Many of the Meetings have been in Germantown, Philadelphia, both on Sundays (First-day Meetings) and on Thursdays (Fifth-day Meetings) at Germantown Friends School, as student and teacher. But I have also attended Meetings—the list is alphabetical —in Algiers, Algeria; Baltimore, MD; Burford, U.K.; Cairo, Egypt; Calcutta, India; Cambridge, MA and U.K.; Cape May, NJ; Casablanca, Morocco; Charlbury, U.K.;

Chicago, IL; Gdansk (Danzig), Poland; Haverford, PA; Leningrad, USSR; Lisbon, Portugal; Maine (various places); Moscow, USSR; New York, NY; Oxford, U.K.; Paris, France; Pasadena, CA; the Poconos, PA; Radnor, PA; St. Louis, MO; Santa Fe, NM; Seattle, WA; Washington, DC; and Whittier, CA (yes, Nixon's Meeting, more or less).

And, even though I'm not very "religious," whatever that may mean, and have trouble with the word and concept "God"—or "god"—I'm still steadily into the risky business of Quaker Meeting.

A Caution

Most of the various utterances and happenings that I report in this book I did not experience myself. They were told or written to me by others, Friends and non-Friends. Some are very hard to tie down, to say exactly where and when they happened. They are authentically said to have taken place in Meeting X and also in Meeting Y—perhaps even Meeting Z. After all when something funny or amazing is said or written, enjoyed, and told and retold, who knows where it will go from there? I therefore caution the reader by telling two non-Quaker stories.*

> Two supposedly senile men were committed to an institutional home near the sea. They were taken out one morning for a walk, accompanied by an attendant, Albert. As they strolled along the shore, a seagull flew low and let drop a blob of excrement which landed right on top of the bald head of one of the elders. Albert saw what had happened and said in great concern, "Wait right here. I'll go in and get some toilet paper."
>
> As the attendant ran toward the building, one elder turned to the other, pointed toward Albert, and said, "He's a darned fool. How stupid can you get? That seagull will be a mile away by the time Albert gets back with the toilet paper."

So where does a story go? And who really knows where a story comes from? Read this about a mysterious distant voice.

> Ernest and Herbert were religious doubters but had just a little faith. Perhaps they were Quakers. They agreed that the one who died first would make every effort to communicate with the other. One day, after a lengthy illness, Herbert did die. For a long time Ernest kept alert, hoping to hear from Herbert. Finally one night he awoke from a deep sleep and heard a familiar voice calling, "Ernest! Ernest!"
>
> "Herbert!" cried Ernest. "You've done it! I heard you! Tell me, what's it like?"
>
> "Well," said Herbert, "it's not bad. I'm in a very comfortable, calm, dark place. After enjoying sleep, I come out and eat in beautiful green meadows. Then I have a little sex and go back into my dark comfort. After a lovely sleep, again I feel hungry,

---

* These are taken from my book *A Treasury of Humor—More Than One Thousand Anecdotes on Everything from Airplanes to Zoos*, 1990; Ivy Books (a division of Random House). To order a copy, call 1-800-733-3000. Price: $3.95. (Major credit cards accepted.)

so I have some more lovely green food to eat, and then a little sex, and then back again to sleep."

"Golly," said Ernest, "so that's what Heaven is like!"

"Heaven?" said Herbert. "Who said I was in Heaven? I'm a rabbit in Altoona, PA."

There is a Quaker Meeting only twenty-five miles from Altoona, attended mostly by human beings.

Some Uses for This Book

I hope the main use for *Quaker Meeting: A Risky Business* will be to provide you, the reader, with some delights: inspiration, provocative questions about humankind, provocative and varied answers to those questions, and some good laughs or deep, silent chuckles. Also, as I was writing it occurred to me that there is a goldmine of themes and statements for preachers of sermons in any denomination. Also people who have to make speeches or be entertaining at parties, or even amuse their spouses or parents or children, may find ammunition (whoops!—that's not a very Friendly word) for their purposes.

The Index

There is a detailed index of subjects, people, and even special Quaker phrases which will increase the usefulness of the book.

Chapter I: Quaker Meetings, What Are They?

Before we get into the risky business of Quaker Meetings, let's consider in a straightforward way just what they are and how they work. My Germantown Meeting in Philadelphia describes Quaker Meeting for Worship in a leaflet for Friends, attenders, and visitors. Here, in part, is what it says.

A Straightforward Explanation

Our Meetings, which are without program, clergy, music, or offerings, are based on silent waiting upon the Spirit, reflecting our Quaker understanding of the nature of the human relationship to God. This manner of worship has

Germantown Meeting at Germantown Friends School, Philadelphia, grades 7-12 present. (Eric Johnson is the fifth person from the left on the facing benches.)

been a reverent practice since the Religious Society of Friends arose as a Christian expression in the mid-Seventeenth Century. Friends believe that every human being is endowed by God with a divine spark, a Light Within, that enables each to know God's will directly, and so...our worship...leaves each free to search for God in his or her own way, and free, too, to share the fruits of reflection in vocal ministry (speaking) as God leads.

This same Light Within is seen by Friends as endowing human life with sacred quality, so that it may neither be debased, nor exploited, nor destroyed for any reason... This is the source of Friends' social testimonies: our pacifism, our concern for...social justice, and for the relief of suffering. It is the source, too, of our belief that all persons must be free to develop fully their own capacities and live lives of integrity, simplicity, and service...

Quaker Meetings, Many Meanings

Here is the way a well-seasoned Friend, Leonard S. Kenworthy, sees Quaker Meetings for Worship.* Meeting for Worship can be:

- *a confessional* where I open up to the Divine my sins and shortcomings;
- *a spiritual gymnasium* in which I wrestle with my well-being and that of others, striving to release new sources of energy;
- *a philosopher's study* in which I search for the meaning of life and my place on this planet;
- *a nursery or garden* in which I plant seeds and nurture them;
- *an architect's studio* in which I plan my life;
- *an accountant's office* where I tally my assets; striving to use these resources wisely for myself and the world;
- *a vast mural* in which I paint in vivid colors...people, books, events, and movements...which have enhanced my life;
- *an historical museum* where I view and review the high points in the history of Christianity and of other world religions;
- *a stained-glass window* in which each of us present is a tiny and unique part, bound together...through our shared silence and our shared messages;
- *an orchestra*, with a wide variety of instruments, which produce beautiful music when...played under the direction of The Great Conductor;
- *a launching pad* for social concerns;
- *a holy of holies* in which we as worshipers push aside the curtain of our busy and often hectic lives and enter into a special place where we...listen for words of forgiveness...encouragement, and...wisdom from The Great Source of Light and Love.

---

*Leonard Kenworthy is the powerhouse behind—and in front of—Quaker Publications, and World Affairs Materials, Box 726, Kennett Square, PA 19438. Write to Quaker Publications for other materials about Quakers and related subjects.

Quaker Meetings: Source of Energy—a Catholic View

Leonard Kenworthy writes of Meeting for Worship as a source of energy. This is well attested to by a Catholic publication, *The Quakers,** by William J. Whalen, Associate Professor of Communication at Purdue University, and a Roman Catholic. Dr. Whalen does not suggest the "risky business" of our Meetings. That will come later. Here are excerpts from his pamphlet:

- All the Quakers in the world add up to fewer people than the Catholics in a diocese such as Peoria or Dubuque. Yet the 198,000** members of the Religious Society of Friends have demonstrated for more than three centuries how a small band of men and women can witness to the world out of all proportion to their numbers.
- Since 1943, Quakers have maintained one of the most influential lobbies in Washington, D.C. Their Friends Committee on National Legislation opposes capital punishment, conscription, and military spending while supporting peace, the sharing of the world's resources, and human rights.
- Recognition of Quaker activities on behalf of peace came in 1947 when the Nobel Peace Prize was awarded jointly to the American Friends Service Committee and its British counterpart, the Friends Service Council.
- Most Quakers show only a slight interest in winning others to their faith; at times in the past, some groups of Quakers have devoted more attention to purging the membership rolls of those who fail to meet some standard of conduct than to spreading "the Truth." The 118,000 American Friends comprise one of the smallest components of the American religious panorama.***
- What distinguishes the Quakers from many other Christians is their personal commitment to God and humanity. The Quaker worships God by serving Him through society. Although decidedly mystical, Quakerism does not understand a purely interior religion. It believes that the Christian faith must express itself in action and service.
- Quakers consider the Bible to be a word of God but consider the Inner Light to be a manifestation of God. The same spirit of God which inspired the writers of sacred Scripture can enlighten the individual seeking Christianity today.

---

*Claretian Publications, 221 West Madison Street, Chicago, IL 60606; 1977.

**As of 1990, the number of members was just over 216,000.

***Some Friends seem to have taken the world's overpopulation problem personally and to have begotten very few children. One Friend I know, in order to counteract this situation, has suggested a Five-F Committee: the Committee For Fertility and Fecundity For Friends. Another agile-minded Friend, knowing the Quakers never have enough money to pay for all the good works they get involved in, responded that it should be the Eight-F Committee: the Committee For Fertility and Fecundity For Friends Financially Fixed and Funded.

- The Quaker withdraws to the silence of the weekly Meeting only to find spiritual nourishment and inspiration and to go back into the world. There is no such thing as a Quaker hermit or a Quaker monastery where contemplatives isolate themselves from the world and its affairs.
- At the time of their beginning, about 1650, the Quakers refused to serve in the army or navy, swear oaths, pay tithes for the support of the established church, doff their hats to others, or use honorific titles. They usually branded the Anglican clergy a "hireling ministry," and sometimes heckled preachers in their pulpits. They made enemies. The established church saw Quakerism as a threat to true Christianity, and the state saw the Quakers as obstreperous critics and rebels.
- Fox* himself was imprisoned eight times, for a total of six years. Between 1650 and 1689, more than 450 Quakers died in prison for their religious beliefs.
- One of the most famous Quaker converts, William Penn (1644-1718), came to Philadelphia in 1682. He was the son of an English admiral to whom the king owed a large sum of money. He settled the debt by giving a charter to the son, who had become a convert to Quakerism. This was a large tract of land west of New Jersey. William Penn thought of calling it Sylvania but the king suggested he call it Penn-Sylvania. It became a haven for Quakers and a center of religious freedom in the colonies.
- Naturally their pacifism kept the Quakers out of active participation in the American Revolution. Quakers who did serve the colonial cause, such as flag-maker Betsy Ross and General Nathanael Greene, were disowned.
- One Quaker farmer is said to have addressed his recalcitrant cow at milking time: "Thee knows that I will not swear at thee. And thee knows that I will not strike thee. But what thee does not know, cow, is that I might sell thee to a Baptist who would beat the devil out of thee."
- All but two of the Quaker colleges in the United States were founded since the Civil War. Best known of these colleges are Swarthmore, Earlham, Haverford, Guilford, Wilmington, William Penn, Friends and Whittier.
- This small denomination has contributed two presidents of the United States—Herbert Hoover and Richard M. Nixon. The latter once told a *London Observer* reporter: "On my mother's side of the family, we were Quakers. Her name was Milhous and she came from a Quaker family that left County Kildare in Ireland in 1729. My father was Irish, too. His family was Methodist, but when he married my mother, he became a Quaker." Nixon never worshiped with the Quakers in Washington while holding the posts of congressman, vice president, or President, and declined to meet with fellow Quakers who suggested a pastoral visit.

---

*George Fox, the "Founder" of the Society of Friends (1624-91).

- If Quakerism has anything to tell Roman Catholics it may be that personal commitment is central and essential to the Christian faith. The Quakers are mystics but they do not ignore mankind in cultivating their own spiritual lives. As William Penn wrote: "True godliness does not turn men out of the world but enables them to live better in it, and excites their endeavors to mend it."

Note the verb "excites."

So Where Is the Riskiness? Some Samples

From what I have written so far, Quaker Meetings (and Quaker actions) sound like good and powerful happenings. And so they are, much of the time. Often if a Friend has missed Meeting on Sunday (First Day), she or he will eagerly ask someone who went to Meeting. "So what happened in Meeting today?"

Let me give a few examples of what happens in this risky business. Feel perfectly free not to agree with the headings under which I've grouped them.

Comical.

G.K. Chesterton (1874-1936) once wrote: "The test of a good religion is whether you can make a joke about it." One could also add "or tell a humorous story during the service." The Society of Friends passes this test well. And it passes despite the very "sober" people who started the movement. For example, Robert Barclay (1648-1690), the nearest thing to a Quaker theologian we have, wrote in his book *An Apology for the True Christian Divinity as Preached by the People Called, in Scorn, Quakers* (1676), that it "is not lawful to use...comedies among Christians, under the notion of recreations, which do not agree with Christian silence, gravity, and sobriety: for laughing, sporting, gaming, mocking, jesting, vain talking, etc., is not Christian liberty, nor harmless mirth." However:

- Haverford College is an excellent Friends' institution near Philadelphia. A graduate writes that in the early 1950's the student newspaper had been full of indignation about the College requiring attendance at Meeting for Worship on Thursday mornings. "You had to be there, check in and attend, or you were in trouble with the Dean. There had been a lot of talk, yet we all dutifully let ourselves be checked off, not wanting to get in wrong with the Dean.

  "So there we sat, often silently steaming with indignation. Then, out of the silence, William Bacon Evans, a well-known character on campus and our most visibly and eccentrically quakerish Quaker, stood and uttered these deathless words: 'Once there were two skeletons in a glass case [silent titters at this] and one turned to the other and said, "You know, if we had any guts we would get out of here!"'

  "The poorly stifled reaction was deafening. But no one left."

- A "weighty" Friend in a well-established Meeting had a tendency to preach (not just speak) at length almost every Sunday. Also, he often paused in mid-speech to await further Divine guidance. One morning after he had preached a great length, he paused and murmured, "And what shall I say next, Lord?"

From a back bench a voice, not Divine, answered clearly, "How about 'Amen'?"

- A Friend spoke in Meeting about how dangerous it is for us to allow our religious words, or even our silence, to become a mere form, without deeper meaning. As a non-religious example of the ridiculousness of rote utterances without conviction he told two true stories.

   He said, "A small brother and sister, members of a high church, had grown very fond of a pet sparrow, which finally died. They decided to organize a formal interment for the sparrow. So they went out in the yard and dug a grave. Their mother watched and listened, fascinated by the proceedings. They wrapped the sparrow in cloth and the boy intoned, 'In the name of the Father, the Son...' and the sister interrupted, dropping the sparrow into the grave, saying, 'and in the hole he goes.'

   "Another example of rote recital, perhaps by the same siblings, was overheard by the mother. The children were practicing the liturgy of the church. The girl recited, 'In the name of the Father, the Son, and the Holy Ghost...' and she paused. At once her brother continued, 'and the Republic for which it stands.'"

This comical message, with a more than comical meaning, led to a truly moving Meeting for Worship, "gathered" around the theme of sincerity and false piety.

- A Meeting for Worship in Wassau, Wisconsin, was being held in the home of a local Quaker whose house during the day was used as the offices of the local Historical Society. One of the residents of the house was a mynah, a bird whose powers of mimicry excel those of parrots. Friends settled into worship. Then the telephone rang in another room and the mynah screeched, "Historical Society." This happened several times, but Friends worshiped on. At last, a Friend rose from the silence and began to speak, only to have the bird call out, "Aw, shut up!"

Outrageous

- At a Meeting in Cambridge, Massachusetts, which tends to be visited by Harvard and Radcliffe students, several young people stood in fairly rapid succession and gave vent to their personal feelings and anguish about a number of non-religious subjects. Then an older Friend stood and said **"These young people who have spoken should know that in Quaker Meeting our verbal ministry is supposed to come forth because we have a direct pipeline to God. Well, I must say, and I expect God will agree, that the messages we have heard so far this morning stink of the pipes."**

- In a Meeting for Worship at William Penn Charter School, Philadelphia, a student stood and declared, **"I am the Messiah,"** and sat down.

   After a moment, another student spoke: **"Don't strive for mediocrity."**

- In the mid-fifties at a Meeting in Barnesville, Ohio, a man stood up and removed all of his clothes, while saying loudly, **"We should be as we are! We should be as we are!"**
- Perhaps fifty years ago a Friend in Germantown Meeting, Philadelphia, had a tendency to speak too frequently, too lengthily, and rather incoherently, even though it was evident that he knew his Scriptures well. At last, the elders of the Meeting agreed that the next time he spoke, two members should usher him out of Meeting. The next Sunday, he did begin again to speak. After a few minutes, the two designated Friends arose and quietly walked over to him. They grasped him firmly by the elbows and propelled him toward the door. As they did, he looked around, glared at the worshipers, and shouted, **"Our good Lord Jesus Christ rode into Jerusalem on the back of one ass. I am being carried out of Meeting on the arms of two."***

Inspiring or Wise or Both

- At Hartford, Connecticut, Meeting, a Friend stood, looked about, and said, "In most churches, temples, and places of worship, you will find words on the walls, over the altar, emblazoned in stained glass windows: words from the Bible, words Jesus said. In this room, there is only one word: Exit. In Latin that means He (or she) goes out. And that is what we do. We go out to make real in the world the messages and the peace we have received in this Meeting."**

- During this hour I have been watching the sunlight streaming in this room. Most of us nearly all the time take the sun for granted, never giving any thought to it. What a marvelous thing it is, 93 million miles from our Earth, 110 times the diameter of the Earth, with 10 million degrees of temperature at its core. All these scientific facts seem impersonal, until we realize that the universe with all its suns and galaxies is the fruit of God's Being, and is under the care of God. The whole universe, including ourselves, is within God. The Quaker poet Whittier said it truly:
  > I only know I cannot drift
  > Beyond His love and care.

- In a fairly large Meeting near Washington, D.C., Friends had found themselves troubled, and sometimes bitter, about disagreements among them. One Sunday, after

---

*This story has been reported to me as having happened in several Meetings. Who knows? Also, on the next First Day—it was a warm spring day—the Friend did not come to Meeting, but halfway through the period of worship his voice was heard emerging loud and clear from all over the Meetinghouse. He had gone down into the basement, opened the door of the furnace, and preached directly into it so that the sounds came out the registers, of which there must be about twenty.

**A similar thought was expressed, perhaps a bit tritely, in Burford Meeting, England, near Oxford:
"May we not be like porridge,
Thick, stodgy and hard to stir,
But may we be like Cornflakes,
Crisp, fresh and ready to serve."

about fifteen minutes of silent worship, a Friend rose and said, "We know that each person here can speak and be spoken to directly by God; that if we wait in silence we can hear the still, small voice. This voice can invade us, can *unite* us.

"We know that there is an eternal spirit, 'which was before the world was,' a spirit that many of us call Christ. This spirit was beautifully and perfectly exemplified in a man called Jesus. From studying his life, accepting his way, and worshiping his God, we can be guided, comforted, excited, and filled with joy.

"We know that in each of us the spirit of Christ can be born. When we speak and act in accordance with the example of his life, but in our *own* circumstances, we are Christ's instruments, God's instruments; we know that in his spirit we can walk cheerfully and with power among the people of the whole world, of our nation, of our Meetings.

"We know that neither God, nor Jesus, nor the Spirit of Christ, can act now in the world, except through *us*, that, in the words of St. Theresa of Avila (1515-1582), 'Christ hath no body but yours, no hands but yours, no feet but yours.' And from this knowledge we know that *we* must do God's work.

"May this knowledge unite us!"

- Sometimes Friends utter a spontaneous prayer in Meeting, but not as often as in earlier years when, if a Friend prayed, all of the members rose at the words, "Oh, God..." or "Dear Lord, we pray..." Here is a prayer uttered in Germantown (Philadelphia) Meeting by a Friend, a Friend trained in the ministry but who left his church many years ago because he found the Quaker testimony of pacifism spoke to his needs. He prayed:

  "Our God, who art the loving parent of us all, visit us, we pray, this morning. May we know by hearts that burn within us that Thou art 'closer to us than breathing, nearer than hands and feet.'

  "Oh God, look into our imaginations and cast out what is impure and unworthy. Look into our minds, and fill them with decent and unselfish thoughts. Grant us determination and courage each day, each moment, to know and to do Thy will."

- "We need to be unafraid of risk and to be courageous. Caroline Shipley, who was undaunted by anything in life, was walking down Market Street (Philadelphia) one day. A youth tried to snatch her voluminous bag. Quickly, she caught him by the shoulder—she was a very strong woman—and said with a firm smile, 'Let's sit down here on the curb and talk about this.'

  "She came home with her bag. The young man went off amazed and smiling.

  "Friends, we must all learn to sit down here and talk."

So: Quaker Meeting: a Risky Business—inspiring, funny, outrageous, thought-provoking, encouraging—and energizing. Now let's look more extensively into what happens in Quaker Meetings.

Quaker Meeting: A Risky Business

Chapter II: Some Outrageous Meeting Happenings

We shall now look more deeply into what happens in Meeting, but as you read, do not forget that Meeting for Worship is much more often a profound and inspiring experience than an outrageous one. This is shown in Chapters III ("Holy, Inspiring, Mysterious Utterances") and VIII ("Gathered Meetings"), as well as parts of other chapters. Now to the amazing and outrageous.

- In the aisle seat on the men's side of the Meetinghouse was Thomas Potts, the perennial Clerk of the Meeting, whom I recall primarily as a Presence. He was almost invariably seated when we arrived at the Meetinghouse. He would then close his eye and let his chin settle on his chest at exactly 10:30 A.M. He would sit motionless until, without glancing at a clock or watch (we youngsters watched him like hawks, hoping to catch him sneaking a peek). Exactly at 11:30 he would raise his head, look

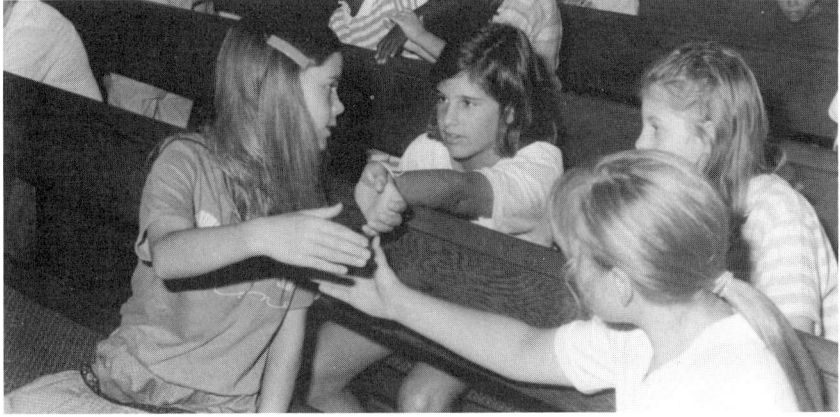

Breaking meeting at Friends School, Haverford, PA

around and then turn to Stanley Yarnall, who usually sat to his left, and break Meeting.

You should know that "break Meeting" means to signal its end by shaking hands. It has nothing to do with destroying anything. After the Meeting-breaker shakes hands with his or her seat-neighbor, Friends and attenders generally shake hands with all of those within reach. Then come announcements and the greeting of new attenders, who are asked to stand and identify themselves so that after Meeting "we all may give you a more personal greeting."

- One morning, as I was going into my usual restaurant, two men were being ejected. From their behavior and by their inability to walk, it seemed obvious that they hadn't quite made it home from the night before. Or maybe they believed in getting an early start. Whatever, they were obviously drunk. After some minor commotion they left. The restaurant quieted down and I had breakfast. I then went on to Meeting. On time.
  Since it was a very warm early spring day, the Meetinghouse doors were left open. I was sitting near the door when, about halfway through the Meeting, I heard someone on the outside say, "There's no one here. Let's go in." It was the two men from the restaurant. They seemed a little surprised when they saw all of us sitting there, but they came on in and sat down. The Meeting for Worship continued, and a few people delivered messages. Whether or not either of the two men had any previous experience with a Quaker Meeting, they seemed to get right into the swing of things.
  Finally, right before the Meeting was scheduled to be broken, one of the gentlemen got up and gave a good ten minutes of what a Freudian would call "free association." He lost me quickly. However, even after all these years, I still remember how his message ended on a great note: "My mother is dead, I don't have any teeth, but I'm happy."

Wanderers into Meeting sometimes do cause amazing things to happen. Here's an anecdote from 1949.

- In 1949, I was in Annapolis, Maryland, in connection with American Friends Service Committee work, and on First-day morning I attended Friends Meeting. It was held in a small auditorium on the campus of St. John's College.
  I was surprised to find only two other people there. After about thirty minutes I was moved to speak. The split second I sat down one of the two young men whirled around in his seat, strongly and argumentatively expressed strong disagreement with what I had said, and appeared then to expect me to respond immediately. I, however, said nothing.
  At the rise of meeting, I shook his hand, and inquired whether his mode of reaction was usual in Annapolis Meeting. "Search me," he said, "I've never been here before."

"At the rise of Meeting"? That's another Friendly way of saying "end." People stand up, shake hands, and talk, person-to-person with no Divine element, except as we are all, all the time, children of God. And here's an example of how childlike even adults can be. The happening occurred in 1936.

- A German Friend had left his native land because of the political and economic turmoil that followed World War I. He had emigrated to the United States and had sought out Germantown, a section of Philadelphia, assuming that at least a vestige of his native culture persisted there. Despite his mistake, he stayed, established a link with Germantown Meeting, and managed to find odd jobs, some for members of the Meeting. Then came the Depression; he could no longer find work, and he began venting his growing despair in long, incoherent sermons, week after week, which left all Friends exhausted.

  One Sunday morning he was the first to speak, and there was an audible groan from those assembled as he rose to his feet. I happened to be watching Thomas Potts, Clerk of the Meeting. He opened his eyes, rose to his feet, and started down the aisle towards the German Friend, with every eye of the Meeting upon him, except those of the speaker himself. The man wasn't aware of Thomas's approach until the Clerk reached the end of his bench at which time he stopped in midsentence as if confronted by Jehovah Himself. Thomas kept coming, laid his hand gently on the German's arm, and the two of them sat down together. There then ensued the most deafening silence that I have ever experienced in Friends Meeting.

Restraint, or restraining, in Meeting is something that has happened—and happens—from time to time, although, proportionally speaking, rarely. Here is an ancient, overseas example.

- At the Friends Meeting in Tokyo, Japan, about 1910, Gilbert Bowles was, as were other leaders and elders, seated on a low platform in front of the main Meetinghouse benches. The weather was cold, so a round iron stove between the platform and the benches where the attending folks sat was kept fired up.

  Each of the benches had a long wooden strip placed at the level where the rather short Japanese could place their feet during Meeting. The stove was stoked (coal and wood) by the janitor of the Meeting who also served as keeper at the gate leading to the big compound where the Meetinghouse and the Friends Girls School were. The janitor's name was Kin, which translated means "gold." "Kin San," as he was called, was sitting on the bench near the stove.

  On one particular occasion Kin was tapping his heels on the wooden footrest. Then Gilbert Bowles came down off the platform and said quietly to Kin San, "Please stop tapping your heels."

  Kin San paid no attention to the request but kept right on tapping quite loudly. Gilbert stood it for several minutes and then, since the warning had made no impression, came down off the platform and picked Kin San up bodily and carried him outdoors. Kin San made no noise, and the whole episode was conducted in silence. The usual meeting continued.

  Kin stayed out that Sunday. He behaved properly at subsequent Meetings.

And here is another happening, perhaps holy, that occurred in Germantown Meeting during World War I. It was a great-uncle of mine to whom it "happened."

Some Outrageous Meeting Happenings

- In Meeting for Worship, about year 1916, George Warner, an Elder of the Meeting who rarely spoke, found himself suddenly "moved" to speak about the saving power of Jesus. *And*, for no reason known to him, he was inspired to speak in French. After he had given his ministry, and after Meeting had broken and Friends were puzzling over why George Warner had spoken in French, a young man came shyly forward and shook George Warner's hands. In French he told Warner that he was sailor from France and had been given a period of liberty at the Port of Philadelphia. He had taken a trolley car and gotten off on Main Street, and was then wandering through Germantown. He saw an interesting looking building and just walked in and sat down. He said that he had been feeling like "a stranger in a strange land," far from home and in despair, even contemplating suicide. Then he entered the Meetinghouse, heard George Warner's words *in French*, and felt restored. "I now know I have something to live for," he said (in French). He was invited to the Warner home for Sunday dinner, after which, a restored person, he returned to his ship.

The next happening occurred also during World War I, in 1917, in the worship part of Yearly Meeting at Arch Street, Philadelphia.*

- An elderly Friend from North Carolina was present. Somehow he got started on the subject of inscriptions on tombstones. He went on and on quoting inscriptions: "*Requeiscat in pacem*; Here lie the mortal remains of ...; Remembered by his devoted wife and children; His soul goes marching on; The grave itself is but a covered bridge leading from light to light; Peace at last; Graves are the footprints of angels; May many an evening sun shine sweetly on my grave; Gone to another Meeting; We are thankful for her life and all of those touched by her love; The grave buries every defect, covers every defeat; Proud even in death, here to rot in state; The monuments of noble men are their virtues...."

  After he showed no sign of stopping, one of the men on the facing bench said to him, quite distinctly, "Friend, I think thy message would be more appropriate at another time."

  But the Friend heeded not and kept right on. After two or three minutes more of this, another Friend, together with the man who had spoken first to the inscription reciter, each took one of his arms and escorted him out of the side door. This did not deter him, and we could still hear him for several minutes, in spite of the closed door.

Obviously one of the main risks of a Quaker Meeting is that those in silent worship will be seen by some people as a wonderful, quiet audience, ready to be preached to. A few years ago, in Philadelphia and its neighborhood, a middle-aged man, Robert—not a Friend—started coming to Germantown Meeting. Here is what he said in essence but usually at great length, and time after time.

---

*In case you wonder why many of the events recounted in this book take place where they do, remember the person who, when asked what Quakers believe, said, "The Fatherhood of God, the Brotherhood of Man, and the Neighborhood of Philadelphia."

- "The world needs peace! You Quakers are not doing enough about it. The people of America, of the world, are not doing enough about it! We are about to be destroyed by war. The only man who saw this clearly was the great savior of the world Dwight Eisenhower, the great general, the great President. We need to follow his ideas and learn from the great things he did.

    "So I have started an organization, The Peoples of the World United for Peace. Everyone is joining. You all should join, for otherwise, unless we take urgent action, unless we remember Dwight Eisenhower, we shall be destroyed. Destroyed! And all because we...."

And so Robert would continue at great length. In some Meetings, Friends would slowly stand in silent protest, for it was the umpteenth time they had heard this and Robert would say, "You want to stop me! You cannot! The Peoples of the World United for Peace...." As far as anyone could discover, Robert was the only member of the POTWUFP.

Robert was so persistent and lengthy that he drove people away from whatever Meeting he happened to be concentrating on. He was a danger to Quakers. Our Meeting in Germantown, after months of weekly First-day anguish, decided to station someone outside the Meetinghouse to stop Robert from coming in, to speak lovingly to him, and invite him—very firmly—to come with them to the Meeting office where they could talk. This worked pretty well. The person or persons who were appointed as Robert-stoppers came to be known affectionately as the "goon squad" for that day.

Once, before the "goon squad" was established, an elder member of the Meeting, who fairly often used to recite the Lord's Prayer ("Our Father which art in heaven, Hallowed be thy name...") and then interpret various parts of it in ways that gave it fresh meaning for today, when Robert was speaking at great length, rose from his seat, went up to him and said firmly, "Robert, people have told you that you are damaging our Meetings for Worship. I want to say, too, that you are interfering with my constitutional right to the free exercise of my religion." That, Friends remember, shook him, but not enough to stop him next Sunday.

Another man—it seems to be males rather than females, doesn't it, who are the causes of risk to Meetings—came frequently to Germantown Meeting. His skull was severely dented in front from some sort of radical surgery. The operation seemed to have left him occasionally mentally unbalanced. Here are the sorts of utterances he would rise and make in a strong, resonant voice.

- "On my way to Meeting, after I had taken a shower and gotten dressed this morning, I had a very important thought. Oh, hell, all your complacent faces have driven it from my mind. I'm leaving." [And he marched out.]

- "I want to know just one thing. Will somebody tell me how I can make myself go home and paint the windows of my house?" [And he marched out.]

- "This Meeting is disgusting! Look at you! The hope of the world is in its youth. I look around and all I see is a lot of ugly old people." [And he marched out. I remember this occasion especially vividly because it was the Sunday of the weekend that members of my class at Germantown Friends School were celebrating their fiftieth reunion, and many of them had come to Meeting for Worship for the first time in many years. It took more than a little explaining to make it clear that Quakers were not going off their rockers, although most of them were so deeply convinced of the importance of Meeting to the life of the school that they understood the freaky nature of this happening.]

This case has a happy ending, I'm glad to say. After a number of weeks of non-attendance (much to everyone's relief), the man came to Meeting again. I could almost hear people, including myself, groan. He sat down. Meeting began with about ten minutes of silent worship. Then two or three Friends spoke well, with good periods of silence between their messages. As I remember, the theme was love and caring. But *then*—groan!—the man stood up, looked around at all assembled, and said quietly but clearly and slowly: "**I want to make an offering to this Meeting. I offer you my apologies; my gratitude, my prayers—and my** *silence.*" And he sat down and worshiped with us.

Sometimes in Meeting one Friend will speak of something another member of Meeting said.

- A seasoned member of our Meeting, whose name I shall not say, recently wrote to a group of men who were planning a fiftieth reunion of an American Friends Service Committee workcamp in the Tennessee Valley Authority area in 1938. His words were: "I've kept my membership in the Society of Friends, which has profoundly influenced me, but for many years I never went to Meeting. Now I attend, within moderation. I find the silence comforting and the company agreeable. But God bores me."

Why, I wonder, does God bore him? What did he mean? Especially in recent years, some Friends have tended to be impatient (even bored?) with religious fundamentalists. One told this experience in Meeting.

- I was flying on a plane next to a man reading the Bible. Now and then he said very audibly, "Amen!" Finally, I turned to him—I probably shouldn't have—and asked, "Are you a preacher? You sound like one."

    "Yes," replied the man, "I am. We are all sinners and we should read God's Holy Word and believe!"

    "Do I gather," I asked, "that you want to save souls from Hell?"

    "I do, I do!" he said.

    I'm afraid, then, I couldn't refrain from asking him, "Well, friend, then why don't you go there?" [laughter in Meeting]

    The rest of our flight was spent in silence, and my question to myself since then has been: Do we ever serve a good purpose by using rude language?

More than once over the years I have worshiped in Meeting, I have heard a Friend begin his or her message by addressing God. "Lord, did you read in this morning's *New York Times* that...?" or even to address queries to the Almighty, such as, "Does it not seem paradoxical to Thee, O God, that ...." Well, who knows? Perhaps God does get puzzled; perhaps God does need to be kept abreast of events by a *Times* (or *Inquirer*, or *Globe*, or *Post*, or *Herald*) subscriber. Perhaps only thus can God know about the doings of God's wayward children.

Sometimes one of the risks during the silence of Meeting for Worship is bodily utterances other than vocal. Some Friends fall asleep and snore, or grunt. But more frequently, even though we are told that the Inner Light is deep within us, and that we should "center down," and obey its still, small voice, what is heard is not a voice. It is also far from still or small. I refer to the rumblings of the human digestive process.

What to do when the stomach—or the elongations below it—are audible? Does one sit quietly and hope that most Friends will think it is someone else? Does one quickly shift position so that the way will be opened? This problem is well enough known so that it was the subject of a letter published in the *Vermont Castings Owner's News*, Summer, 1985. Here are excerpts:

- You need to be advised that the use of your wood stoves may be hazardous to religious observances.... I am a member of a small Quaker Meeting.... After Meeting we have a potluck meal.... In the winter ...as people arrive, they put their dishes on the stove to keep warm. Inevitably, about half an hour into our silent meditation, the aroma of the foods warming...reaches those in Meeting. About five minutes later the rumbling of stomachs will be heard. About ten minutes of this is the longest even the weightest Friends can stand without some sound emanating from their mid-sections....*

But now let us go from a warm subject to a cold one. Sometimes a most unlikely thought can start off a good Meeting for Worship. One such thought is *slush*. A Sunday in January, all around a large eastern city Meeting, it had snowed some six inches, and then warmish temperatures had turned the snow into a mucky mess. A Friend rose and said:

- My thoughts this morning are dominated by slush. Slush raises a number of interesting, even spiritual questions. Slush is moist and cold. In the streets and gutters it is dirty. When a car passes by going too fast, slush splashes and we, the splashed on, become moist, cold, and dirty. You should see my trousers now!

---

*Some Friends have mixed feelings about noise in Meeting, as suggested by this verse an Oxford, England, man recited during a too-vocal Meeting for Worship:
    Thank goodness for the motorbike,
    that makes a roar next door.
    I can't hear our Friend's declaiming,
    and he can't hear me snore.

Slush has no form, no character. It has no convictions, except superficial ones, as when, after a brief period below freezing, it thinly crusts over. We walk on the crust—in faith—and break through, filling our shoes with glop.

And yet slush is flexible. It can be reformed (reborn?) into ice—hard and reliable—or water—wet and ready to flow out of the way and let us Friends get on with our good works.

Friends, let us ponder. Is there anything good to be said for slush? How many of us are like slush? In what ways are we slush?

Quaker Meeting, a risky business. Believe it or not, this slush utterance gave rise to what Friends call "openings," and a wonderful Meeting for Worship followed. And this leads us to the next chapter, from the outrageous and amazing to utterances mysterious, inspiring, even holy.

Chapter III: Some Insights; Messages about Children; Dramatic Experiences; the Nature of God and Jesus

Most of the messages quoted in this chapter were sent to me by others who knew that I was working on this book. They all arose from different Meetings for Worship, and there is no particular unity among them. They are excerpts from a process. I have arranged them into groups for easier reading.

Insights

- There are two kinds of Friends in our Society, and two kinds of people in the world: the <u>therefore</u> people and the <u>however</u> people. <u>Therefore</u> people say, "We need to deal with the problem of hunger in poor countries and in our own country. <u>Therefore</u>...," and they go on to say what actions they will undertake. <u>However</u> people make the same beginning statement but follow it with, "<u>However</u>...," and they explain why nothing can be done.

  Try it for yourself after each of these statements: "We must improve race relations in the city of Boston...."; "This morning I decided to volunteer at least two hours a week in our neighborhood nursing home...."; "I am amazed at the amount of litter dropped in our city parks...."

  We need fewer <u>however</u> people in the world and among Quakers. We need more <u>therefore</u> people.

This was said by Henry Joel Cadbury (1883-1974), Professor of Divinity at Harvard, chairman of the American Friends Service Committee and one of the translators of the Revised Standard Version of the New Testament—a *therefore* person if there ever was one!

Henry Cadbury's words were quoted in Charlbury Meeting near Oxford, England, and a world-famous Oxford scientist, doctor, and radiologist, Frank Ellis, responded thus:

Some Insights; Messages about Children;
Dramatic Experiences; the Nature of God and Jesus

Drawn by Jean Price Norman

- I am interested in Henry Cadbury's words just quoted, and I agree that we need more people of action. However (if I dare use the word), it seems to me that, at least when we think about problems or try to discover solutions, we <u>therefore however</u> our way toward truth. That is, whenever you think you have proved something ("<u>therefore</u>"), some conflicting evidence tends to raise its head ("<u>however</u>"). Thus we properly "<u>therefore/however</u>" our way through life. My own aphorism is: There is no substitute for brains. Unless you know what you aim at, you can't get there. Idealism is more real wisdom than Realism, in the long run. Aim for the ideal or you won't reach it.

The same Frank Ellis expressed his religion or philosophy (and in the Society of Friends, the words "religion" and "philosophy" often are used interchangeably) thus:

- The difference between human beings and other living creatures is the ability to reason.
  By virtue of such reason, we have learned more and more about the secrets of the universe of which the earth is a small part.
  "God" started everything. All things obey "natural laws" as far as we know.
  Therefore, that of God in every one is the ability to reason logically.

Another British Quaker, Ronald Pinfield, when he learned that I was writing this book, from time to time sent me some "Pinfield Ponderings." They might well have been—and most of them probably were—uttered in Meeting for Worship.

- Whilst I was shaving this morning, listening to the radio in the background, the birds outside singing, this idea came to me:
  All life is based on COMMUNICATION. Think for a moment about words, letters, books, talks, speeches, radio and television, the telephone and the satellites, the Morse Code and all human expressions.
  Nature, also, is full of communications, the birds and all insects, the fish and mammals in the sea. Do you know that whales and dolphins communicate with

each other across distances of hundreds of miles? The whole creation never is still. It is going on all the time.
> The sun that bids us rest
> Is waking our brethren neath the western sky.
> I hear it in the rushing breeze,
> The hills that have for ages stood,
> The echoing sky, the roaring seas,
> These prompt our song that God is good.

And here is another Pinfield Pondering.

- One's mind is like a camera, as we snap the pictures here and there. It is recording those memories that slip back into the subconscious mind. They remain there within Man's own computer, the brain which stores all those things of knowledge.

  I came to this conclusion one day as I was pondering and looking back over my life, of all the knowledge of things implanted within my own brain. When I was in the pharmacy, I was taught to recognize the drugs by smell and appearance and their reactions chemically, and what they were used for. Also their importance in being poisonous or not.

  When anyone came into the pharmacy and asked for the medicament, I knew immediately where to go for it, amongst all the thousands of different little things in that store. Why? Because it was stored in my computer, and when the brain was tapped, it reacted immediately. The mind is a wonderful thing. It remembers going back over time and bringing back into consciousness those events and things stored within. Sometimes the mind remembers things that we would rather forget, but if we feed the mind with beautiful things, then those memories will be sweet and beautiful too. God's mind?

This "pondering" reminds me of an amazing happening that occurred, not in Meeting for Worship, but during an episode of surgery. It was told about in a Meeting.

- Paul McLean is a "brain geographer" at Johns Hopkins Hospital in Baltimore, Maryland. McLean was operating on a woman aged about fifty, who was born in Germany. She had left Germany at age six, and had not spoken German since she arrived in America. She "knew" no German. But the woman had epilepsy, and one of the ways to cure a person who has epileptic seizures is to find out what part of the brain is affected, and then to make an incision there. In order to do this, the surgeon does a trepan: he lifts up a section of the skull to expose the brain, and then he excites different parts of it with an electric needle so that the patient, who is fully conscious, can say, "Yes, that's the spot."

  As Paul McLean was applying his needle to carefully selected areas of this woman's brain, he excited the language area. There was an amazing result. While this area was excited, the woman who in "real life" spoke no German, responded to the surgeon's questions in German—at about a six-year-old level. When the excitation was removed, she knew no German. So: What miraculous things do we have stored in our brains?" "God's mind?" Who knows God's mind? Perhaps it is a condition, or a presence, or something created by <u>our</u> mind but somehow beyond yet within it.

Here are the words of a Friend at a small midweek Meeting in Cambridge, Massachusetts. They were spoken by a woman who knew she was dying of cancer.

- I have been aware of that place of love and peace within us. It is there just beneath the surface of our consciousness. It is there to uphold us, and we can go to that place whenever we wish.

When this woman died, a Meeting for Worship was held to celebrate her life, and many, many people attended, people who had been affected by her work as a teacher of art, as the manager of a large miscellaneous household of seekers, as wife and companion of a world-famed Harvard psychologist, David McClelland, and as mystic. She was my first cousin, and during the memorial Meeting, I recalled an event of our childhood.

- When Mary and I were about eight years old, we were climbing in a rather fragile, many-branched tree. At one point, I got a little frightened and said to my cousin, "Mary, we'd better be careful. We might fall down."
  Mary replied, "Well, maybe, but we might fall <u>up</u>."

Are we responsible for what goes on in our minds? This question was the subject of several messages in Germantown Meeting. A Friend stood and said:

- I live in a house with woods and grass on three sides and a major city street at the end of a lane. Sometimes during the day, but especially at dusk, suddenly the air is rent by the roar of motorcycles racing up and down Ardleigh Street, their mufflers cut out. The peace and quiet are ruined, the patients in a nearby nursing home are disturbed, and the utter violence of the roaring cycles enrages me.
  One evening I had a fantasy of how I would like to die. I would secretly build a high wooden tower, higher than the woods, with a clear view to Ardleigh Street. I would buy a machine gun and mount it atop the tower. Then I would climb the tower and when a cycle went by I would pull the trigger and shoot at the rider—not at his tires, not at his cycle, but at his head. I would kill him! And I would keep on killing motorcyclists until the police were called. They would rush to the tower and climb it. I would go on shooting cyclists to stop their Devil-inspired noise until the police pulled their guns and shot me dead.
  Yes, I actually imagined this scene and my pleasure in killing the noisemakers and my feeling of glory as I died for a noble cause: the right to silence. These feelings were in my mind—the mind of a Quaker, a pacifist, a person who believes in non-violence, who was a conscientious objector during the war, who would never do violence; who—as with Gandhi or Jesus—would rather be killed than to kill.
  And yet I had these feelings—this fantasy—in my mind. It shows, I think, that we are not responsible for our feelings. We are responsible only for our actions.

And we cause ourselves vast and needless worry and burden if we feel responsible for our feelings. It's what we <u>say</u> and <u>do</u> that we are responsible for.

Sometimes Friends are moved by a recognition of the wonders of nature, small and great.

- I was in the garden this morning working away, and on the path sat a little Blue Tit. It had just come out of the nest box that I had put up. Here it was looking at the new world around it, taking stock of it all.
  Wondering if he was remembering what his mum had told him, "Beware of strangers," I approached slowly. He was only as big as my thumb, and here I was a giant, six feet tall, peering down upon him. He <u>did</u> remember what Mum had said, and he hopped away into the bushes.
  Is this how God sees us? He holds us in the hollow of His hand. He sees the meanest sparrow fall in the street.
  Tennyson wrote:
  > Flower in the crannied wall,
  > I pluck you out of the crannies,
  > I hold you here, root and all, in my hand,
  > Little flower—but if I could understand
  > What you are, root and all, and all in all,
  > I should know what God and man is.

  Or David, the Psalmist: "Thou has made man a little lower than the angels, and has crowned him with glory and honor."
  Friends, I shall be looking out for my little Blue Tit friend and watching his progress. His family have been around a long time.

- If we put the clock back in October thus ending summer time, it is a device for saving daylight. But we cannot do that with life. Life is a continuous process, as night follows day. We would at times like very much to put the clock back in our lives. This is not possible. Life must go on, and often too swiftly. Time seems to catch up with us, or even overtake us when we are least expecting it to do.
  Nature is not dying in October as winter approaches, life is going back into the root, ready for the resurrection in the spring, the season of new life and new experience. This then teaches us that life and death and resurrection are all part of our experience. As Paul said in his letter to the Philippians, "To live is Christ, and to die is gain."

- Botanists tell us that in the autumn the sap is retreating down the stem and trunk to root, retaining energy for life for the following spring. I feel like autumn at times. I lose my sap and die back, retreat into myself, saving my energy to wake again for spring, to come back again with renewed vigor bursting forth to life.

And where does out vigor come from. Should we take credit for it? An eighty-year-old Friend said late in Meeting, from the very back row of the Meetinghouse:

- Everything I have comes from someone else—my food, my language, my love, even my body. Therefore I owe me to everyone.

And how do we keep from feeling discouraged when so often life seems to bring us—or others—bad luck? Out of a Meeting that had been worshiping and pondering this question, a Friend stood and said:

- Yes, often we are discouraged by fate, by bad luck. We think that, to use an unFriendly image, the cards are stacked against us. But, to change the image, we should remember a simple matter of probability. If we are flipping a coin, and if for the past nine flips the coin has come up tails, the chances are fifty-fifty, no more, no less, that on the next flip it will come up heads, no matter what!

A Friend, who had been looking around at all the faces in the Meetinghouse, many of them so familiar to her, arose and stood silently until the eyes of most of the attenders were fixed upon her. Then she said two plain sentences.

- Friends, we really do not know each other. We only bump masks.

This led to a profound and deep silence.

Children

In Chapter VI, you will read about some troubles, glories, behavior, and even messages from children. Here, however, are some messages *about* children.

One Sunday a baby girl who had been carried, sleeping, into Meeting, soon awoke, and, despite the best efforts of her mother, cooed, then whined, and then started to cry. This "vocal ministry" was clearly disturbing to those present, so the mother handed the baby to her father, who arose and carried her toward one of the doors. Just as they were about to go out, the baby, who was facing the Meeting, looking over her father's shoulder, smiled and said in a strong little voice, "Bye-bye!"

After a moment of amused silence, a Friend rose and said:

- That young person who just left us gave, all unknowingly perhaps, a most important message, "Bye-bye!" What does it mean? It means, "Good-bye." And what does good-bye mean? It means, "God be with you!" What a deep and meaningful wish for us—that God should be with us! It's a good message for all of us to tell each other.

Some older children, present in Meeting beside each other on bench, moved this Friend to say:

- I see, before me, a row of beautiful, young people. Thank goodness for these young people.
  I hope that they will grow into a clear consciousness of the one abiding, eternal, universal Reality—and that is—God: universally attached to all of life, universally

participant in all the joys, and in all the sorrows, of all creatures, human and non-human; ever present, ever giving, ever receptive, ever loving—the bedrock of our faith.

Later, when the Friend communicated with me about what he'd said, he explained that the message was "an expression of my view of the centrality of God in worship, as distinguished from the emphasis on Christ, which some other Friends give." "I have always had this view," he said, "long before I became associated with the Quaker Universalist Fellowship, which I helped to found."*

I, too, have trouble with not only the emphasis on Christ—even though I wrote a book, *An Introduction to Jesus of Nazareth—a Book of Information and a Harmony of the Gospels* **—but also with the idea of God, and especially "the Lord" (masculine). I remember one Sunday morning at breakfast, when I was thinking about Meeting for Worship, and God, I suddenly said to my wife, "Gay, if thee were asked to describe God, what would thee say?"

She looked surprised, then thoughtful, then modest, but after a moment of thought she said slowly, discovering the words for the first time, "I guess I'd say God is a creative transforming harmony." Wow! I've always gotten comfort and enlightenment from that.***

But let's get back to children, to babies. Bonnie Hosie, a member of Las Cruces, New Mexico, Meeting, writes about a Welcoming Meeting for her newborn child.

- Our small meeting had already gathered in silence when my family quietly took our seats in the circle. We were a few minutes late, but tender smiles from a couple of Friends made me feel welcome. In my arms lay our 11-day-old son, Isaac.

    This was his first appearance at Meeting for Worship, yet he had been very much with me through worship many Sunday mornings. My husband, John, held Jacob, 2, on his lap. Caleb, 6, sat on the other side of Isaac and me. I unwrapped the baby's blanket and unzipped the light blue bunting that both my older sons had worn, and I smiled at my youngest child. Isaac stretched and settled himself into the familiar comfort of our worshipful silence.

    My heart began beating very fast. I felt short of breath. Shaking, I stood slowly and held Isaac out before me. I was powerfully moved as I began to speak:

    "This is our new son and brother Joseph Isaac Rhodes-Lutheran. He was born at 12:04 A.M. on December 2. He feels very comfortable here in this circle. He

---

*Address: Quaker Universalist Fellowship, c/o Sally Rickerman, Box 201, R.D. 1, Landenberg, PA 19350; phone: 215-274-8882

**An Introduction to Jesus of Nazareth* is no longer in print, but I have a number of copies. You may have one by sending $15.20 ($13.95+$1.25 postage) to Eric W. Johnson, 6110 Ardleigh St., Philadelphia, PA 19138

***Later I realized that the initials are ACTH, which are the initials of a hormone of the pituitary gland that stimulates the production of sexual hormones and adrenalin, among others. The real name is adrenocorticotropic hormone, so perhaps it's better to stick with "G-O-D"!

has shared the quiet strength of this meeting with me for many months. The joy I felt then, beginning to know him, holding him inside of me, I hope you will share now as each of you holds him and with words or silence welcomes him into this community of Friends."

I passed my peaceful child into the arms of a Friend to my left. In the fullness of this moment, tears flowed down my face. Wonder and joy held all of us as we passed this new life from the cradling arms of an elder Friend into the wiggly embrace of a youngster.

And in a Meeting for Worship at Stony Run, Maryland, someone spoke of the true test of love for a child:

- An ancient Sanskrit legend tells of a holy man who was asked to decide which of two quarreling women was the real mother of the child and should therefore get the baby. He directed each of the women to take one of the baby's arms and legs and to pull, a sort of tug-of-war. When the baby cried, one of the women let go. The holy man decided that she was the real mother.

    This legendary story should help us decide what to do in the difficult situations we face today, when change is taking place faster than we can absorb it. We must demonstrate the feelings of the real mother, and let love and sympathy and mercy determine our decisions, rather than the desire to win a tug-of-war.

The real mother of the child obviously showed a superior sort of "intelligence," not the mere IQ intelligence. A Friend spoke one day in Meeting about our narrow view of what intelligence is and how this penalizes youngsters who aren't taught "the basics" well.

- There are many varieties of intelligence. A friend of mine, Sally Scattergood, was working with a group of fourth graders at the Pastorius Elementary School in Philadelphia, and she was concerned that children, often obviously bright and creative, did not know enough reading to do well on standard mutiple-choice tests.

    One boy, when faced with a question and four squares in one of which to X an answer, took a moment to join the squares ingeniously with lines to make a wonderful surrealistic picture of a rabbit.

    "And," said Sally, "when I looked at his scores later, he didn't do half badly! But he got no credit for the rabbit."

    How many of us, with narrow concepts of how people ought to respond—not just in school, but in life—fail to see the light within people we meet?

Dramatic Experiences

In Meetings for Worship, sometimes very dramatic, even spectacular experiences become a part of the ministry. For example, a Friend told of the following experience of a member of Germantown Meeting, John Emerson, when he was in the armed forces during the Korean War (1950-53). This was before John became a Quaker and a pacifist.

Quaker Meeting: A Risky Business

- In November, 1952, John Emerson served in the Korean War. He was responsible for managing the supplies for a small airforce base just about on the 38th parallel, the line dividing North and South Korea. As a part of his duty, John had to take a flight south to Seoul.

    The plane took off and flew very low over the water, when suddenly one wing was caught by an extra-high wave, and the plane was flipped into the bay, about a mile offshore. John was able to get out of an emergency exit as were many of the passengers.

    For a time, they all stayed near the plane, which was the accepted practice, so that they would be more likely to be rescued. But as John observed the plane, he saw that it was slowly sinking. He looked toward the shore and, against regulations, decided to swim for it. For a while he was swimming well, but the waves were immense and there was a strong undertow. John was pulled below the surface several times and barely made it to the air again, gasping for breath. He was becoming totally exhausted and said to himself, "I can't do it. I'll just have to let myself drown." He went down again and remembers that suddenly he felt his feet touch a sandy bottom.

    The touch of sand gave him a new surge of energy, and he struck out again for the shore with fresh strength. Then he noticed some people on the coast, who were waving their arms and cheering him on. Thus invigorated he made it to shallow water and struggled up onto the beach, saved.

    He looked back toward the plane and saw nothing. Later he learned that it had sunk and that all of the crew and passengers were drowned.

    John remembers his feeling of sadness, but also the feeling of renewal when his feet first touched the sand. Sometimes a miraculous bit of encouragement can save our lives.

    As a result of his experience, he refused to fly again on the next plane, and had to travel on small railroads, through great discomfort, to get back to Seoul.

    What can we learn from this experience? First, perhaps, that sometimes it's better to use one's own judgment and go against regulations. And, second, that a slight touch of sand on the foot can give us energy and life that we thought were lost forever.

    We need encouragement and new surges of life—and we should find ways that we can give them to others.

Another tragic war that the United States was in was the Vietnam War, 1954-75, a tragedy for the people of the USA and even more for the people of Vietnam. In 1967, at a world gathering of Friends at Guilford College, Greensboro, North Carolina, there was a large Meeting for Worship, and a speaker raised the question, "How relevant is this gathering, and the Society of Friends, to the really deep problems of the world?" The speaker then said:

- I am a soldier in Vietnam, crawling through the jungle with orders to kill. And I can't hear you.

    I am a mother of eight in an inner-city ghetto. My children have no food. I can't hear you.

Some Insights; Messages about Children;
Dramatic Experiences; the Nature of God and Jesus

And later in the war, about 1972, my mother, Edith Warner Johnson, wrote a poem titled "Vietnam." It was read in a Meeting for Worship at Haverford.

- VIETNAM
  In the valley of death seeded with bombs,
  Valley of burnt-out rice paddies, of scuttling rats,
  And escaping, perishing people, we lay among our wounds
  And those other wounds we had inflicted.

  "Buddha," you moaned, petitioning his monumental presence
  To bend in pity of your suffering.
  "Jesus," I cried, seeing his cross, hearing again his words,
  "Let this cup pass from me."

  We turned and faced each other, searching through
  The crater crevices of our pain. I saw in you myself,
  You saw in me yourself. Our hands reached out, touched
  With unburdened ease as we crossed the chasm of our diversity.

  Caught in the labyrinth of death and time,
  For us now there was one country, one loyalty to every man.
  In our dying we spoke the triumph and the truth of the unsaid,
  Piercing words, words of the resurrected dead.*

And the reader asked, "Must we die together in the valley of Death to cross the chasm of the world's diversity?"

Sometimes a dramatic experience is in a dream, and its aftermath:

- Last night I had the most vivid dream I have ever had. I dreamt that I picked up the <u>New York Times</u> from our front steps and saw that the entire front page was taken with a two-word headline in enormous print: WORLD ENDS.

  I awoke in alarm and gradually realized the world was still here. And I look out over all of you, and I know that in reality the headline could more accurately have said, for each of us: WORLD BEGINS, NOW!

Sometimes, as with John Emerson in the ocean off the beach in Korea, we have an experience that makes us feel that for us the world will end—for us. A speaker said:

- Most of us too often take life and living for granted. In the summer between 11th and 12th grades, four friends and I drove west to see some national parks. For a

---

*A book containing 121 of Edith Johnson's poems, titled *Strange Country*, can be bought by sending a check for $14.00 to Eric W. Johnson, 6110 Ardleigh St., Philadelphia, PA 19138. This includes postage and handling. The poems range from witty and sassy to deep and moving. There's nothing particularly "Quakerish" about them.

few days, we stopped in Glacier National Park, in Montana, a park that straddles the Continental Divide. We hiked up to a rather narrow ridge right on the Divide, and there we cooked and ate our supper and were resting. Suddenly I had a crazy idea. To the north I saw a small, rather dramatic looking minor peak, perhaps seven hundred feet above where we were camped, and I decided simply to take off, run up to the top and then come right down again. I said to my friends, "I'm going for a little hike," and set off.

The climb up to the top was easy, even though there was no trail. The surface was fairly smooth and rocky.

Soon I reached the little summit, looked around, and felt exhilarated, but then I realized that the sun was low on the horizon and that a cold wind was coming up, so I started to hurry down. In a few minutes, I came to a ledge that I hadn't seen before and was aware that this wasn't the same route I'd come up on. However, it was obvious that I should go on descending, so I did—by means of a fairly narrow, steep chute between two rocks. I slid down the chute and landed on another ledge, a very narrow one. I looked all around and saw that the ledge led nowhere, and that I was rimrocked. So I would have to clamber back up the chute to where I had been a minute ago.

But when I tried to go up the chute, I found that the rock was too smooth and the chute too wide for me to make my way up. I just kept slipping back to the rim. I paused and looked all around. About three hundred feet below the rim was a boulder field. If I fell off the rim, it was certain death on the boulders. I was very frightened. I looked down to the ridge below where my four friends were, very small, in their sleeping bags. I looked to the west: nothing but the setting sun, ranges of lower mountains, and rivers and streams, all of which would end up eventually in the Pacific. I looked eastward: the same sort of view, and all the waters that way would end up in the Gulf of Mexico. I felt extremely small, and also I was beginning to shiver, both with fright and from the cold wind. "I have to get off this rim or I'll freeze to death," I thought.

I looked back up to where I had just come from, and suddenly I saw a grassy-edged rock, perhaps twenty feet above me, and I realized that if I reached that grassy edge, I'd be all right. But how to do it? At the eastern end of the rimrock was a fairly smooth, steeply-inclined boulder which ended at the top with the grassy edge. But at the lower end of it was a drop into nothing—down to the boulder field. I had no choice. I carefully moved my body onto the boulder, grasping every nitch and rough spot with my bare fingers and pressing the toes of my boots in each crack. Slowly I made my way upward, but just before I reached the grassy edge, a pebble came loose under one of my boots, and I began sliding very slowly downward, down to the three hundred foot drop to the boulder field. No matter what I did, I kept very slowly sliding, until I felt one boot toe go over the edge. But at the same moment I saw, just to my right, a small sapling rooted in a little crevice. I reached out my hand and very gently held the sapling—it couldn't have been more than a foot high. But it was firmly rooted, and I stopped sliding.

I panted and gasped and then, <u>very gently,</u> using the sapling, worked my way back up the boulder. I passed the sapling, and extremely carefully chose each fingerhold and toehold, and pressed my body hard to the rock so as not slip again.

At last I was able to reach one hand up to the edge of grass and hold onto it. It was solidly set in the rock, and I pulled myself up over the edge. There I was in a little alpine meadow—safe!

I stood up. I looked east and west, and then down to my now-sleeping friends. I raised my arms and gave a shout of exultation. Never, never had I been so grateful for life—for being alive.

I now saw the way down, the way I had come up, and within ten minutes I was back on the ridge. I crawled silently into my sleeping bag, filled with a new joy of living. It wasn't until a couple of days later that I dared tell my friends what a fool I had been, how near to death and—now—how glad for life! I'm not sure they understood.

So friends, be glad to be alive!

The next experience is a less spectacular drama, at least on the surface. A young woman, mother of four school-aged children, rose early in Meeting, looked around at us all, and said:

- Friends, I need your prayers and support. It may seem like a small thing, but for the first time in our married life my husband has had to go away for ten days. I am feeling alone and overwhelmed.

Immediately there came into my mind a short poem my mother had written about when my father walked out the door one morning to go to work in town. As he left, he turned back to my mother. I explained this to the Meeting and then said the poem:

- When today, you said on departing,
  "I'm <u>going</u> now, but remember I'm not <u>leaving</u>,"
  Your brief words shook the horizon,
  Multiplied into a tender rain falling on meadows
  Where I stood knee-deep in joy.

After Meeting the young woman came up to me, gave me a hug, and said how much my mother's words had strengthen her.

A member of my Meeting, Lou Paulmier, was a splendid physical education teacher at Germantown Friends School, and he had been a football star before that. Lou was strong, agile, graceful, and expert. But a few years ago he gradually became affected by Parkinson's disease. He had to quit his physical education job and now, helped by his wonderful wife and grown children, works as Caretaker of the Meeting and School. He often has a hard time to walk about without suddenly seeming to trip or fall or stagger, and his speech is somewhat affected, but none of these things daunts him, and he courageously goes about his work with love and care. One Sunday Lou stood up in Meeting, full of strength. He said:

- People who are sick or in trouble help each other. I want to tell you about the death of small-f friend who would have made a good large-F Friend. He was Bill

Worrell, a beekeeper. He helped me a lot. But he loved bees. He collected them and then would take swarms of them to people who had hives and could use them. He lived his life to be helpful, and I loved him.

After that Meeting, someone said to a small group of us, "Wasn't that wonderful, what Lou said!" We all agreed, and then she went on, "Do you know what Bill Worrell had on his bumper? It was a sticker that read, 'Beekeepers don't die. They just buzz off.' "

An American Friend who, with his wife, spent a year in England, visited a splendid Renaissance-style house, set in a hugh park landscaped by the famous Lancelot ("Capability") Brown (1715-83). One of the features of Longleat is what is said to be the world's largest, longest maze, covering a couple of acres with twists and turns, and, in the middle, stands an 18-foot-high wooden step-tower with a platform on top. You pay a pound or so to enter the maze, but, once in, you have to find your way out, at dusk—or, if you're in distress and you call for help. You are then shown the way out, for a rather hefty extra fee, I understand.

This American Friend was attending Jordans Meeting the next Sunday. Jordans was built in 1688 and its burial ground contains the remains of William Penn, the founder of Pennsylvania, and his wives. On this Sunday there were many visitors at Jordans because of some kind of tour. After a long period of silence, the American Friend stood and said:

- Have any of you here ever been lost, truly lost? A few days ago, my wife and I entered the world's longest maze at Longleat. We enjoyed ourselves as we turned corner after corner, curve after curve, choosing each time the path forked. We were trying to reach the wooden tower in the center of the maze. We were told that once at the tower we could easily find our way out. From time to time we got close, but then the path forked, and we could not get to the steps of the tower. We had been trying for over half an hour, even marking the path where we had been, or alternately turning right, left, right, etcetera, at each fork, but we never reached the tower.

    Finally we decided to quit trying to reach the tower but just to find our way out because it was getting late in the afternoon, but we couldn't find our way to the EGRESS sign. We passed a worker who was trimming the maze hedges. But when we asked him how to get out, he said, "It's easy, just turn left three times, then right twice, and then you'll see."

    We tried that, but before we knew it we were back beside the worker. This time he said, "For a quid I'll show you out." We weren't going to do that! So we walked on, turning and forking, for another twenty minutes, and suddenly I felt a sense of disaster. "We are lost!" I said to my wife. For the first time in my life I was lost, helpless, and no matter how much we applied our intelligence, we could not get out. I felt humble, stupid, put down.

    But then we remembered that all we needed to do was to call for help. However for a moment I thought—felt deeply—how terrible it is to be lost! And how many people in the world are truly lost and have no way of getting help.

I think it is important that all of us at some time have the experience of being lost!

As this thought invaded my mind and spirit, and as we were still walking the maze, suddenly we spied a sign, "This way out." We were found, directed, free again!

A few minutes after the Friend had spoken, there was the sound of small voices and feet outside the Meetinghouse, and children started coming from Sunday School to join the big Meeting. But there were so many people attending that day that the boys and girls were lost. A seasoned member of the Meeting rose and said with a smile:

- Our American Friend has spoken movingly about the importance of being lost sometimes in our lives, but perhaps now is not the time for our children, and Jordans Meeting is not a maze. Therefore I suggest that parents of children stand for a moment so that families may be reunited and worship may continue.

There was a chuckle, parents stood, children smiled gleefully, and after a brief scamper, the spirit of worship was restored.

The Nature of God, Christ, Jesus

Although many Friends are not very religious in the conventional sense of the word, they do think, and sometimes speak, about God, Christ, and Jesus. Some will say "Christ," some will say "Jesus," but few say "Jesus Christ." And we have already read about the Friend who liked Meeting but was "bored" by the subject of God.

In one Meeting, a Friend, who, while remaining a Friend, also joined the Catholic Church, said this.

- St. Ignatius [c. 800-877], bishop of Antioch and a Christian martyr, said that there are three voice inside you—your own voice, the voice of the good spirit, and the voice of the evil spirit. I find this a thought-provoking idea, and I suggest that perhaps our main task in life is discernment—to discern which voice we are hearing, that of the evil spirit, of the good spirit, or our own voice? On that discernment we should base what we say and do.

Here are some messages about God that Friends have given in Meetings for Worship. You will see what variety there is in Friends' views, even though they exist together—for the most part—in harmonious appreciation of differences.

- God is our home—and we have a homing instinct. It's like the child's game where one child chooses a spot in the house or yard and then the other children search for that spot—or maybe Spot,—the only clue being, "You're getting warmer"; "you're getting colder," etc., until some child finds the spot.

    Take the case of a bird called the brown cuckoo. The female lays her eggs. Then she migrates four to five thousand miles, and her eggs—and then babies—

are adopted and sat on and kept warm by other birds, not cuckoos. After about six weeks, the babies grow up, learn to fly, and they migrate too, and join <u>their own parents</u>—in some mysterious manner. How do they do it? How do they find "home"? How do we find home?

There are other times and ways to feel we are at home with God.

- At eventide as we walk through a wooded glade, we see the shafts of sunlight breaking through the canopy, we hear the song of chaffinch on yonder bough, we make leaves rustle under foot, disturbing blackbirds fleeting down woodland path in full cry. The rabbit trotting to the left shows the little flagged tail, and the pheasant calls at the edge of the wood. We gaze at hoists of bluebells, red campion, and yellow primroses, and know sweet odors perfume the air. The rustling breeze sweeps down to bend the stems of grass. We stop to hear the babbling brook.

    Yes, this is peace away from madding crowd at eventide. I turn and see on a log across the stream an old man sitting. I join Him, take off my shoes, and with Him dangle my feet in the cool water. I feel His strong arm about my shoulder and know at last that I am Home with Him—at eventide.

Friends are often interested in, and deeply respectful of, other religions' views of God. One quoted a "hymn" of a group of Pygmys, a small people of equatorial Africa, generally under five feet in height.

- Here is a Pygmy Hymn. What can it teach us?
    In the beginning was God, today is God.
    Tomorrow will be God.
    Who can make an image of God? He has no body.
    He is the word that comes out of your mouth.
    That word! It is no more.
    It is past, and still lives.
    So is God.

And what about Hindu gods? One of them is Shiva, god of destruction and regeneration. A Friend in Burford Meeting, near Oxford, England, told of an experience after World War II.

- When I was in India, a Hindu friend said to me while we worked together in the Pay Office, "I won't be in the office tomorrow. It's my God's birthday, the Hindu God Shiva. But I would like you to come for dinner at my house in the evening."

    I thanked him very much and met him the following evening and went to his house. We had a very nice meal full of exotic spices and fruits of eastern culinary. After the meal, Hari Om Prakash, for that was his name, said, "I would like very much for you to come with me to the Temple." I felt greatly honored and accepted the invitation.

    We went to the Temple of Shiva in the old city of Meerut. The Brahmin priest was at the door. We greeted him, and I was introduced and went into the Temple, having taken off my shoes at the door.

There was the graven image of stone from the floor to the ceiling. It was my friend Hari's God of the Hindu religion. Hari's eyes were shining. I looked at him and then at the God. I knew Hari. He wasn't worshiping that stone. He was searching for the great Spirit behind the God, bowing down to stone in his search for Truth. I ask this about most worshipers. What are they worshiping?

But some Friends are not afraid to state a strong, probably simplistic, view of God.

- What is God? G, O, D. <u>G</u> for generator, <u>O</u> for operator, <u>D</u> for destroyer. That is what a person I know stated with certainty. Is there truth in that idea? Can we believe that God is a destroyer?

One Friend, however, feels certain that God will provide what we need to do the work we have to do. She said:

- God will not send thee into the forest to hew an oak with a penknife. If he gives thee a task thou never didst, he will give thee a strength thou never hadst.

Before I quote other messages about God, I should remind you of the old story about the young reporter who happened to be in Johnstown, Pennsylvania, during the terrible flood of 1889. He started his dispatch thus: "God sat on a hill here last night and watched disaster and death sweep through this community."

His editor promptly wired back: FORGET THE FLOOD—INTERVIEW GOD.

But now we return to the risky business of Meetings for Worship. A deeply religious Friend, who often states that she holds her problems up to God and feels helped by God's grace, stated:

- Some dear Friends ask whether or not one believes in God or tries to be God-centered. But—what do we mean by God, for Christ's sake!?
  I heard a quotation from Kierkegaard [Soren Kierkegaard, 1813-55]: "There is only one blasphemy—to try to define the nature of God." Even more pithy is the ancient proverb, "If you see the Buddha, kill him!"
  Let us not kill whatever God may be by narrow, rigid thinking.

The question of praying to God is often raised in Meetings. There are many different sorts of messages given:

- You can't always describe your feelings when you pray to God. Do you ever think that God can say <u>no</u> as well as <u>yes</u>? Don't think that you are going to get everything that you ask for; it might not be good for you. You could end up being a spoiled little brat. Well, God doesn't work like that, does He? Lives are certainly different, and God works in many different ways. Talking it over with God may be a way of clearing your mind and getting things into a clearer perspective—seeing the way more clearly, to go forward.

- A couple of months ago I read a book by Paul Davies, *God and the New Physics*. It made me think that cosmology, mathematics, nuclear physics—none of them can prove or disprove the existence of God. But they can offer analogies and metaphors for the spiritual life. Considering the immensity of the universe and of the atom, it has been hard to think of a personal God or Spirit. But if light can be seen as particles or waves depending on the method of observation, so God may be seen as impersonal and personal: If we are in an infinity of time and space which God permeates, then each of us is at the Center and God is there, too, as though all God's attention was on that one Center. If there are different forces—gravity, the electromagnetic force, and the strong and weak forces—which really are different aspects of one unified force, so love may be the human and spiritual expression of that great Unity which is God.

    Also I don't believe that thinking is the sole basis of spiritual truth or experience. But the ability to think is perhaps the most outstanding attribute of our species as human beings and as such it can be an important tool in developing our experience as spiritual beings.

Some Friends, and some attenders at Friends Meetings, are very skeptical about the idea that God will reach down and almost personally do for us what we need with His (or a few Friends say Her) hand. One such Friend told this story in Meeting:

- A very religious man, who had total faith in God, lived in a house by a great river. One night there was a terrible flood and the man had to climb up on the roof of his house to escape being drowned.

    After a time, some men came by in a boat to rescue him, but he refused. "I have faith that God will rescue me." Soon after, another boat came to rescue him, and again he refused: "I have faith in God." Considerably later a helicopter flew over and let down a rope ladder, but the man waved them away, shouting, "I have faith in God to rescue me!"

    At last, the force of the water broke up the house and the man was drowned. He went to Heaven, and when he saw God he asked, "Oh God, God, I had such faith in you, and you let me drown. Why? Why?"

    "What do you mean, let you drown? I sent you two boats and a helicopter, didn't I?"

There are problems about praying to God and thanking God for blessings that we enjoy. Why is it that some live in poverty and misery and some live in comfort, some are killed, some saved?

- Prayer is a strange thing. We pray to God to save us. People, when they are not killed in an airplane crash, like the terrible one a few days ago, thank God for saving them. So why did God not save the others?

    We should not pray to ask God for things, or ideas, or states of mind. We should make our prayers, as Dwight Eisenhower said, "Reporting for duty." God will tell us what to do.

Too many religious people expect that somehow God will reach down and act, and that we must pray for God's action. And many Christians believe that Christ, or Jesus, will Himself act to right a wrong or to bring about good. In the view of many—probably most—Friends, this is not so. Only *we* can act on Earth. In several Meetings over the years, I have heard this conviction expressed through the prayer of St. Theresa of Avila [Spain] (1515-82), who said:

> Christ hath no body or earth but yours,
> No feet but yours, no hands but yours.
> Yours are the eyes to look out Christ's
>   compassion upon the world;
> Yours are the feet upon which He is to
>   go about doing good;
> Yours are the hands with which He
>   will bless us now.

Another Roman Catholic, Mother Theresa (1910-), an Albanian nun who went to Calcutta, Indian, as a missionary at age seventeen, and who won the Nobel Peace Prize in 1979, said strikingly, "To me, every person is Christ." Insofar as Quakers believe in the sanctity of life (which makes many of them pacifists) and know, as George Fox said, "There is that of God in every one," they would agree with Mother Theresa.

But many Friends have trouble with the words "Jesus Christ" said together. They know that Jesus of Nazareth was a man who lived in Nazareth and many of whose acts and words are recorded in the New Testament books of the Bible. They find Jesus's life an inspiration and they try, far from perfectly, to model their own lives on that life. But "Christ" is another matter. The word is Greek *Christos*, and literally means "the anointed." It also means *messiah*—king, deliverer, savior—who will come and save the people of the world, those who believe, from eternal damnation and hell. In this connection, a Friend gave this message:

- In the summer in New Hampshire, I go to a small-town community church where ministers from a variety of denominations preach. One Sunday, a woman Episcopal minister stated her belief that Jesus Christ is our Savior, and the Savior also of all creatures in the universe.

    After church, I asked her, "How can you—or your church—really believe that a single man on planet earth is the savior of the universe?"

    "Well," she said, "I call it 'a scandal of the intelligence.' We have to go beyond our intelligence and <u>believe</u>."

    Can Friends support such a scandal? I ask you. I think not!

Another Friend quoted from St. Patrick (c.385-461):

- Christ be with me, Christ within me,
    Christ behind me, Christ before me,
  Christ beside me, Christ to win me,
    Christ to comfort and restore me,
  Christ beneath me, Christ above me,
    Christ in quiet, Christ in danger,
  Christ in hearts of all that love me,
    Christ in mouth of friend and stranger.

Still another Friend told of George Fox's experience:

- George Fox [1624-91] left the Church of England, and the priests, and became a "seeker." And one day suddenly he had a clarifying inner experience, when he heard a voice saying, "There is one, even Jesus Christ, who can speak to thy condition." When Fox heard this, he later reported, "My heart did leap for joy."

    Soon after this experience, Fox began to preach, and one of his main points was that we don't need the Bible, or history, or the apostles, or preachers, or churches. Christ is within each of us. "What canst _thou_ say?" is what we must ask ourselves.

    And Fox's essential belief can be stated, as Fox stated it in eight words: "Christ has come to teach his people himself"—to teach us, here in this Meeting, _now_.

Then, with a twist, which carried the Meeting forward in an inspiring encouraging way, someone rose and said:

- The greatest failure story in history is the life of Jesus. His life has given millions the courage to fail.

Chapter IV:
The Force of Meetings; Famous Quakers; Noises from the Outside World; Inspiring Words and Thoughts

"The courage to fail"—that doesn't sound like a very forceful idea, but when it was said, it was stimulating and striking. And so it leads us into the start of this chapter, and into its other parts, which rise far beyond failure.

The Wonderful Force of Meetings

Yes, "Christ has come to teach his people himself"—*today*, as I write these words, *today* as you read them.

One of the sentences of Fox that is most often spoken Meeting is this:

- "Walk cheerfully over the earth, answering that of God in every one." That is what we should do, <u>can</u> do, when we leave Meeting today.

Or, again, a Friend well-versed in the thoughts and spirit of Fox said:

- After "heavy inward sufferings," George Fox, according to his journal, "cried day and night" to God. He saw "all the terrible things that are within the hearts and minds of wicked men." And Fox asked God, "Why should I be thus, seeing I was never addicted to commit these evils?" And, wrote Fox, "The Lord answered that it was needful that I should have a sense of all conditions: how else should I speak to all conditions? And in this I saw the infinite love of God. I saw also that <u>there was an ocean of darkness and death</u> [underline added], <u>but an infinite ocean of light and love, which flowed over the ocean of darkness:</u> ...and I had great openings."

- Seldom do I mark a verse in my Bible in red ink. But on a day back in 1971 I did just that.

  The first message given in the Meeting for Worship that morning was from Isaiah: "But they that wait upon the Lord shall renew their strength; they shall mount up with wings as eagles; they shall run and not be weary; and they shall walk, and not faint." [Isaiah 41:31]

  In the long silence that followed, I had the peculiar feeling that there would never be a need to go groping for answers to any problems; it had all been spelled out ages ago by Isaiah.

  I returned home and marked that verse in my Bible—and I find it there whenever I feel troubled.

So often Quaker Meetings are characterized by deep thought and feeling; the silence will speak to someone who needed to be there; someone listened and learned; someone then ran and was not weary; someone mounted up with wings.

- Silence! I hesitate to break the deep silence we have been experiencing, but I am moved to recall some word from various religions—words about silence:

  "Be still and know that I am God."—Psalm 46,10

  "Silence does not make mistakes."—a Hindu statement

  "The tree of silence bears the fruit of Peace"—an Arab proverb

  "Let your silent meditation be on the glorious light of God.

  May this illuminate your mind"—Bhagavad-Gita, a Hindu classic

  "Silence is golden, but the man who practices it is seldom

  seen."—an Arab proverb

  Silence! We feel its power in this Meeting.

- Some Native Americans who came into the Quaker Meeting and saw everyone silent were conscious of the Divine Presence. How do we describe this to the children? One little girl in our Meeting once said, "I listen to the silence, Mummy." Yes, "And a little child shall lead them."

- Meetings for Worship can have such power! Remember, when God rested the seventh day, He was very sensible. He reflected, He took stock, He examined the work he had created. It's a good thing to reflect to look back at times. It's good to have a break, to have a complete change, to meet new people and see new things, also to do new things.

  It has been stated that a change is as good as a rest. Why? Because the change was a very refreshing experience. I have found that Meeting for Worship on a Sunday morning completely relaxes my mind and body. To be still for one hour is in itself a tremendous discipline. I was a manager of a retail store for a national company, and sometimes I brought my work home with me for the weekend, where I could be quiet and think things through and do my planning. But Meeting for Worship for one hour gave me that complete rest. "My chains fell off, my heart was free, Hallelujah!"

- [A world-famous architect said this.] Why did I join this Meeting? I was floating around in the spiritual sky. Then I felt—saw?—an opening in the clouds. Below, I saw a Meeting for Worship. So I dropped through. This is my place!

- For a number of years I was a member of the Middletown Friends Meeting in Lima, Pennsylvania. In that group one of the frequent speakers was sweet-faced, elderly Margaret Taylor. Almost without fail she started her messages with the quotation, "This is the day that the Lord hath made; let us rejoice and be glad in it."

    Her messages were usually quiet and helpful—and varied—and her face shone as she spoke. When she was present and spoke, the Meeting—and our lives— seemed to take on a deeper meaning.

- As I sit in this Meeting [Burford, U.K.] I feel:
    The setting sun comes streaming in through the western window,
        Shadows on the wall reflecting light,
            Rays coming through the window across the room.
    Images dancing as Ghostly figures, as dazzling rays reflect the setting sun.
        The room becomes alive, one watches in breathless inspiration.
            The Lord of the dance is with us!
    Let us go forth and _do_!—and dance.

- Quaker Meeting—this Meeting, today, now!—is a near-perfect combination of introvert contemplation and extrovert action. Here we come, World!

Speaking about Famous Quakers

Occasionally, but not very often, Friends' messages in Meeting quote, or paraphrase, the words of now-famous Quakers, even though there are very few Friends who seek fame.

- We Friends seem to think that we need committees, procedures, and money to bring about social reform and a better world. Let us not forget our own John Woolman [1720-1772], a simple tailor, born in Rancocas, New Jersey who, without seeking it, became famous enough so that the renowned British historian George Macaulay Trevelyan [1876-1972] wrote a special essay about him. He pictures Woolman as a humble pedestrian plodding around among rich slave-holding Quaker families. By his persistence, his sincerity, and his persuasive arguments, he induced them to free their slaves.

    What causes should we today be walking about in the streets for? How many of us are ready, moved by conscience, to be modern Woolmans?

- Fox, when he was released from prison ("the house of correction"), was asked by officials of the prison if he would be captain over some new soldiers to fight for the Commonwealth against Charles Stuart. He refused, saying, "I know from whence all wars arise, even from the lust; and I live in the virtue of that life and power that taketh away the occasion of all wars."

This statement by George Fox led to the famous "Declaration of the Harmless and Innocent people of God, called Quakers: We utterly deny all outward wars and strife, and fightings with outward weapons, for any end, or under any pretence whatsoever; this is our testimony to the whole world."

- Quakerism is not mainly denial; it is asserting the positive. An excellent example of this is the message to Friends that Fox sent in 1656 from Launceton Prison: "...Be patterns, be examples in all countries, places, islands, nations, wherever you come; that your carriage and life may preach among all sorts of people, and to them; then you will come to walk cheerfully over the earth, answering that of God in every one...."

Noises from the Outside World Enter Meeting for Worship

Quaker Meetings are based on silent worship and waiting upon the Spirit. But very often the silence is broken, not by ministry, but by sounds from outside the Meetinghouse. A dramatic example is reported from Germany, in 1940-41, where Friends worshiped deeply even when the sound of the boots of Nazi soldiers marching in a nearby courtyard was often heard.

And I remember, during the years 1952-54, when my wife and I attended Friends Meeting on Rue Guy de la Brosse, Paris, a crowded neighborhood, we were surrounded by narrow streets and tall apartment buildings. Always during Meeting there were the sounds of dishwater being emptied out of windows and splashing on the pavement, of women shouting greetings and comments to each other from building to building—all the noises of streets and life. We had many visitors from other countries, and often, if they spoke, the first sentence would be:

- It is wonderful to hear the sounds of life outside. Our Meeting and our worship should be a part of life....

In England, two Friends spoke these feelings about silent worship and sounds:

- Listen!
  The breeze amongst the grasses sweeping its way across the corn, the rustling amongst the branches or the leaf that has fallen to the ground beneath. The swirl that takes the dust upwards and scatters it around.
  The birds that sing, the sparrow that chirps, and the dove cooing. Raindrops falling, washing the thirsty leaves, tapping the window pane, or dripping from the eaves. The rush of water over the falls and swirling through the rocks. The trickle of the babbling brook.
  The lowing cattle coming home to milk, the sheep in yon meadow, and the cock crowing, sitting on gatepost.
  In Meeting, now, sit and listen in this silence where we are conscious of the unseen God whose voice is so clear to the human soul.

- Yes, it is inspiring to sit quietly in Meeting and to listen to the world outside. The dog barking, the dove cooing, the motor car, and the roar of the motorbike. We hear the fire engine and the police sirens.

    The other Sunday towards the end of Meeting for Worship, a blackbird started to sing. The Meeting was very, very silent. Most of us were listening to its rich contralto voice. It was a beautiful ending to our Meeting.

And at Christmas there are special sounds that we hear, even though in their early days, Quakers did not celebrate any religious holidays. ("Every day is Christmas. Every day Christ is born.") A Friend reported this in a Meeting for Worship:

- The old man was busying himself and humming away a carol. "Have you gone all Christmasy, Graddad?" asked the little boy. I suppose we all get a little Christmasy like Granddad at times. Sometimes we sit quietly in Meeting and our thoughts wander and wonder a little over the past experience of life.

    Christmas is a time to be joyful, to be happy to share gifts; to celebrate with parties and Christmas fare; to sing lots of carols and songs; to rejoice over the birth of Christ, the Newborn King. It's a time for children to be happy and the old folk to feel young again.

    We think of all the celebrations during the year: of harvest and the fall. Praise God for His Creation and the way in which He provides for our needs! Birthdays and weddings, anniversaries and many more.

    In fact we need to get all Christmasy over things!

Another Christmastime experience at my Germantown Meeting is the delight of hearing the little children, in First Day School class across the driveway in the kindergarten building, singing carols, inexpertly, joyously, and with the purity of childish voices. Do these light-voiced children know what deep and inspiring things they sing about?

When I was in Calcutta for the American Friends Service Committee in 1944, doing famine relief work with the Ramakrishna Mission, we had a very small Meeting for Worship in a room of our headquarters at 1 Upper Wood Street. We would sit in silence and hear people go up or down the stairs. Suddenly they would say, "Shhh! There's worship going on in there." And in the room, there was a piano, a hymnal, and a Bible. Friends and visitors, in an unprogrammed way, would feel moved to pick up the Bible and read, or to go to the piano and invite us to sing a hymn.

These Meetings were rich experiences, even though some American Friends could say that the Bible and the piano were "noises from the outside world."

Some Inspiring, Thought-provoking Words Quoted or Said in Meetings

In the last chapter of this book, I shall report on "gathered Meetings," where the silence and the messages—the ministry—made the worshipers feel gathered by the Spirit. Below, however, I cite some messages that were memorable to me, or to others who told me about them. Remember, though, that they were not given in isolation but as parts of a Meeting for Worship.

- [This by an almost totally blind British Friend who, with his family, moved to the very small Scottish Isle of Lewes.]
  FRIENDLY SWANS
  I heard a whooper swan
      Winging towards our lochs,
  Joyfully rejoicing in its faultless flight.
  More like a mute swan I float
  In space and time—in quiet celebration
      Of the dawning light.
  An inner voice more clear, than outward sight.

- At Harvard University, a new library was to be built, and a professor of philosophy was asked for a motto to engrave in stone in the front of the edifice. He chose: "Man is the measure of all things." [Protagoras, 490?-415? B.C.]. Then the professor went on sabbatical, and when he returned, he went to see how the motto looked. Here is what he read: "What is man that thou are mindful of him?" [Paul's Epistle to the Hebrews, 2, 6.]

- It comes down to this: People are to be loved and things are to be used. "Things" include material objects and general principles. Immorality occurs when things are loved and people are used.

- [This prayer, and request to God, is often quoted in Meetings to remind Friends that when they leave Meeting they should go out to make the world better. It was often said in Meeting at the turn of this century by John Wilhelm Rowntree, an English Quaker. "Lay on us the burden of the world's suffering; drive us forth with the apostolic fervor of the early Church."]

  - He drew a circle that shut me out—
    Heretic, rebel, a thing to flout.
    But Love and I had the wit to win:
    We drew a circle that took him in.
    [Edward Markham, 1852-1940]

- Jane Palen Rushmore (1864-1958), a Quaker social worker, at age ninety-four, and always a radical in the best sense, said: "The teachings of our Quaker forefathers were intended to be landmarks, not campsites."

- [This is in a Meeting for Worship, Melbourne, Australia] Yesterday, when our dear friend was about to turn 100, he was asked to stand and talk about it. He rose, there was a long pause, and then he said, "I'm not a hundred yet." How typical of him! He lives—accurately and with spirit—in the present.

- Meeting for Worship can be like a garden [said George Baines, a retired school head at Burford Meeting near Oxford]:

  The shadowy pattern of leaves
  Shaken by this summer breeze
  Breaks the blankness of my paper
  —and my mind—
  Here in this garden of worship.

  Here my shaded soul
  Feels moved by another wind
  And opens out to the Light
  Like these daisies spreading
  Their petals to the burning sun.

  Unafraid, they seem
  To expose their hearts
  But reflect the giving they receive,
  And so teach me
  The value of my insignificance.

- We Friends — and many others — speak righteously about the importance of giving. And that is right: we should give of our time, our means, our wisdom (if any), our selves.

  But often we forget the importance of <u>receiving</u>. We must learn to receive—to receive praise, to receive help, to receive love. Some people who are disabled and could be seen as a burden to those who care for them, are blessed by the gracious way they receive help, and in their receiving they give!

- There is much talk among religious people about the Ten Commandments, as if they were especially sacred. However, when God gave them to Moses on Mount Sinai [Exodus 19: 1-20], God went right on speaking and gave over five hundred more "Laws of Moses"—about slaves, property, temple-building, priestly garments, etc., etc., all as sacred as the Ten.

  And let us remember that when Jesus was asked by a Teacher of the Law which Commandment was the most important, he did not mention any of the Ten but recited two in different books of the Hebrew Scriptures. The first was, "Love the Lord thy God with all thy heart and all thy soul and all thy mind" [Deuteronomy 6:5]; and the second "Love thy neighbor as thyself" [Leviticus 19:18].

- Forgiveness is like perfume from the violet that comes from the heel that crushed it. How able are we to forgive, even when we are made to suffer?

- "The wolf also shall dwell with the lamb, and the leopard shall lie down with the kid; and the calf and the young lion and the fatling together; and a little child shall lead them." [Isaiah, 11,6] It has been said that "Nature is red in tooth and claw" and as we look around we see evidence of this. One animal or bird will kill and consume the other.

In the beginning it was not so for the inhabitants in the garden of Eden. All lived in perfect harmony with each other. Isaiah the prophet recalls this in his words. The predator shall live harmoniously with the victim.

As we look at the world and humanity, we see quite clearly that mankind is also predatory. He lives off his fellows, possibly parasitically, but more than that he, too, is red in tooth and claw. He literally behaves as the animal, the wolf, the leopard, and the lion. But his mind is more sinister. Like a cat playing with a mouse, man's victim or prisoner is tortured. Amnesty International tells us of many countries where this takes place.

What is it in the human personality that makes man like the beast of the jungle? The scriptures say that, "The heart of man is deceitful and desperately wicked." [Jeremiah, 17,9] But why does man behave like an animal? Why should an intelligent being sink to such a level? Did not God when he created us, "set us to have dominion over all creation, the fowls of the air, and all the beings including the beasts of the forest?"

However, man seems not to have risen above the beast, but rather we have become <u>like</u> the beast.

- I am not a socialist, I am not a conservative; I am not a radical; I am not even a Democrat. I am a Contrarian. The purpose of Contrarians is to keep people searching for truth. We should be, as the early Friends were, seekers.

- As I was walking along a New Jersey beach, I saw a woman throwing starfish which had been stranded on the sand back into the sea.

  Another woman passed her and said, "But there are thousands of stranded starfish. What you are doing won't make any difference." The first woman picked up another starfish and said as she threw it, "To <u>this</u> starfish it will."

Some Brief, Inspiring Themes

Many messages in Meeting combine into striking and inspiring themes, or they lead to a "gathered Meeting." Here are two that followed each other. The first was uttered, at age eighty-one, by a world-famous surgeon, and a genius in many fields, the second by the young mother of a new baby girl.

- There is joy in creation, whether in the fields of art, science, or medicine, or whether in the creation of a new life. <u>But</u> when the creation is made, it is no longer the property of the creator or creators. It is out! For example, a work of art must be seen and reacted to; a creation of science will be useful or harmful; a new child will have a mind and ways of his own; new schools or colleges (and many have been created by Friends) evolve far from the founders' statements; a doctor cures a person, but he doesn't ask <u>how</u> the person will use the new-found health—that's up to the person. So there is joy in creation, but we cannot be possessive of what we create.

- Ted and I recently had a baby. What joy! Immediately we started discussing what we wanted our little girl to be like. We made a list of adjectives: loving, happy, considerate, assertive—but we soon found that our daughter was becoming her own self, and that, I now see so clearly, is good. Our influence and dreams are important, but this creation is becoming independent. We cannot possess her.

At many Meetings, it is the practice of Friends to read from time to time one of the Queries.* Queries (in my Meeting) are a profile of the Quaker way of life and a reminder of the ideals Friends seek to attain. Query number fourteen is on Simplicity. Two parts of it are: "Do you keep to simplicity and moderation in your speech, your manner of living, and in your daily work?" "Are you careful to keep your occupation or profession... from absorbing time and energy that should be given to spiritual growth...?" One Sunday after this Query was read at the start of Meeting, there were these responses arising from the worship:

- To keep our lives decently simple, we must learn to say <u>no</u> to some good things we are asked to do.
- If we aren't honest, don't have the simplicity of honesty, our lives get confused and messed up. We must be honest.
- I recently had a day of vacation on a tropical beach. I was alone, alone with the palms, the wind, the sand, the sun, the waves. I suddenly felt the joy of simplicity.

In another Meeting the idea of guilt arose from the silence.

Drawn by John R. Fisher

*A young child asked whether the Queries were those funny-looking people who sat up on the facing benches on Sunday.

- Quakerism, by its nature, makes us feel responsible for more things than we can possibly be responsible for. And so we feel guilty. Let us remember what Thomas Kelly [1893-1941, philosophy professor of Haverford College and author of *A Testament of Devotion*] said: "We cannot be crucified on every cross."
- Quakers have no system to deal with guilt, no ritual, no confession and forgiveness of sins. This may make us more driven to good actions, but we must be careful not to harm ourselves or others. As Cardinal Cushing of Boston said, "Saints are okay in Heaven, but they are Hell on earth."
- You remember in Luke there is the parable of Jesus about the man who fell among thieves and was stripped and wounded. A priest and a Levite saw him but passed by on the other side of the road. Did they feel guilty? Probably not, for they had important things to do. The other day, I saw a man who had slipped on the ice and fallen into the gutter. He cried, "Help! Help!" I passed by, for I had vital work to do at my desk. I feel guilty. I should feel guilty! Guilt is a healthy motivator.

Sometimes there are state lotteries, and people go frantic to buy tickets. They line up for hours at the sales booths. In this connection, a Friend arose in Meeting and said:

- I am astonished at what people tell reporters what they would do if they won. Never have I heard anyone talk about giving money to charity or to a good cause. No, they'll buy a Cadillac, a new house, take a trip, shop for clothes and jewelry— and a few might give a share to their children or parents. But there is never any true generosity.

  If I were to win the lottery, I'd invest 10 percent of my winnings. I'd give 5 percent to each of my three children. And the remaining 75 percent I'd give to Germantown Friends School, the American Friends Service Committee, our Meeting, the A.C.L.U., and about six other charities.

  What would you Friends do with the money if you won, let's say, a million?

This question led to a series of messages on generosity and the responsibilities of having more money than you need to live a plain but good life.

A Friend had been to a small conference of Quaker leaders. At the conference each was asked to write, and then read to the group, a statement on "This I Believe." The Friend explained this and then told his statement:

- I believe in the power of good will; the power that comes if one dedicates one's life to discovering what the good for someone else may be, and sacrificing oneself to achieving that good. This can be called Christian Love; it can be called the Golden Rule. It requires sensitivity, persistence, courage, and a highly developed imagination— imagination actually to picture the situation of another man, whether he be in Philadelphia, Moscow, or Seoul, Korea.

  I believe in sticking my neck out. That is, I have faith that if one speaks out, forthrightly but in a loving spirit, and says what one believes to be true regardless of the consequences, good will result.

> I have faith in non-violence; I believe that war is never necessary and will never solve the world's problems. Further I believe that we should take literally the Commandment, "Thou shalt not kill." To me the life of Jesus, on which I attempt— most inadequately, I admit—to model my own—this life of Jesus was essentially an expression of the power of love, of non-violence, of the futility of physical force used in hateful spirit. I believe that if it becomes necessary to choose between losing one's own life and taking that of another, one should give up one's own, for, in Jesus' words "Whoever would save his life will lose it, and whoever loses his life for my sake will save it." This goes for nations as well as individuals.
> <u>What, Friends, do you believe? Tell us!</u>

This message led to a remarkable series of other messages on the theme of belief. And one Friend said she believed in the health-giving, spirit-raising power of humor, even comedy, in Meetings for Worship. This takes us to the next chapter.

Chapter V: Comical and Humorous Messages

Friends very rarely simply tell a joke in Meeting, but they do quite often illustrate a point or an idea with a humorous anecdote—and this despite the advice from Robert Barclay (quoted in Chapter 1) that Friends must practice "gravity and sobriety" and not engage in "laughing...jesting...nor harmless mirth." In this chapter, I report on some messages and events in Meeting that I hope represent helpful mirth. The first of these concerns an aunt of mine, long since dead, who objected to Quakers who tried too hard to be perfect.

- We Friends can be painfully saintly. It is very hard on those who live with us. In fact, I think it can be said that a martyr is someone who has to live with a saint.
  Let us beware of self-righteousness! It is a risk some Friends run, and it is neither persuasive nor attractive.

This same aunt told me that when, as a little girl, she told her mother, my grandmother, that she was tempted to eat the ripe raspberries off the bushes in the back yard, her mother said, "Marian, when thee is tempted, just say, 'Get thee behind me, Satan.'" But Aunt Marian did eat the raspberries and explained: "I said 'Get thee behind me, Satan,' and he got behind me and pushed me right into the bushes."

Perhaps the best known Executive Secretary of the American Friends Service Committee was Clarence E. Pickett, who served in this post from 1929-1950. He was a witty and inspiring Friend and friend, but he sometime grew a bit weary of Quakers who felt they were always right and doing good. Once he rose in Meeting and said:

- Let me remind Friends that Jesus said, not "Blessed are the righteous," but rather, "Blessed are those who hunger and thirst after righteousness."

A famous Friend, William Bacon Evans, who, as I have reported earlier, always wore plain Quaker clothes and used the plain language (*thee* and *thy*), was a strong pacifist, but also, on the athletic field, a fierce competitor. A Friend told this incident about Bacon Evans:

- Even when our Society of Friends was seriously divided in the Philadelphia area, everyone always welcomed William Bacon Evans because his terse religious utterances and vast fund of wit often shocked his hearers into right-mindedness.
  An example, out in the larger world of non-Friends, was when Bacon Evans was playing soccer for Haverford College against Columbia University. Evans and a Columbia player crashed into each other as they went for the ball. "Jesus Christ!" exclaimed the opponent. "No," said Evans, "just one of his humble servants," and he dribbled the ball away with vigor and, it is said, scored a goal.

In England two of the Friends' schools are The Mount and Bootham. Students from these schools attended Meeting for Worship at York Meeting along with certain inmates from The Retreat, a mental hospital. An impressive, somewhat elderly lady from The Retreat arose and said in a strong voice:

- I have bread ye know not of.

And then she put her hands in her coat pockets and showered the elders of the Meeting with crusts she had taken from the Retreat breakfast table.

Mary Hoxie Jones, daughter of Rufus Jones [1863-1948], the famous Friends professor, religious leader, writer, and activist, reports that a few years before 1955, when the two Philadelphia Yearly Meetings, Orthodox (Arch Street) and Hicksite (Race Street) were united, a well-know Friend spoke at great length at Arch Street. When he was finished, William Bacon Evans rose and said:

- In nearly all Race Street Meetinghouses there are clocks. Sometimes I wish I were a Race Street Friend.

Another incident of overlong speaking occurred at Yearly Meeting. A well-known Friend and respected judge, Albert Maris, was clerk. A somewhat emotionally disturbed Friend stood and spoke at great length. Even after several Friends rose to indicate he should conclude his remarks, he continued. Finally Albert Maris rose on the facing bench and very gently but firmly said, "The Lord is in his holy temple. Let all the earth keep silent before him." Happily it worked and the Friend became silent.

And this reminds me of the remark made by one Friend to another, quite audibly, to another Friend who was hard of hearing: "I'm glad this morning that those who had nothing to say refrained from giving verbal evidence of the fact."

Some Friends, especially scholarly and eloquent (and often inspiring) ones like Augustus T. Murray and Rufus Jones, tended from time to time to speak at length and with vastly interesting complexity. A Friend said about them, "When either spoke, one should have taken his brains with him to Meeting." At one Meeting after Rufus Jones had spoken, an aged woman Friend, who had a voice like a power saw, spoke tersely:

- Jesus said, "Feed by lambs," not "Feed my giraffes."

In this connection, it's nice to know that Rufus Jones startled Haverford Meeting by rising to speak, thus:

- This morning my daughter Mary Hoxie said to me, "Father, I could be more sure you were inspired if you weren't inspired so regularly."

Too-frequent, or too-lengthy speakers in Meeting can be a problem. Quite some years ago one such Friend, who sat on the facing bench, cleared his throat as was his wont before he rose to give ministry. A Friend sitting just behind him heard the throat-clearing and noticed that the man's coattails were hanging behind the bench. So that Friend firmly pressed his knees against the coattails. Thus the speaker was unable to rise, and he kept silent. Later in the Meeting, without clearing his throat, he said:

- I was about to speak earlier in the Meeting, but the Good Man held me down. Perhaps there is a message here for me.

As I have explained elsewhere, Friends generally consider the Bible not as the final word of God. They believe in "continuing divine revelation," revelation from God now. The scriptures are rich, instructive, and beautiful documents and help us to know what is true, but are not The Truth. Thus some Friends allow themselves not to become well-acquainted with the Bible. In this connection a British Friend said, tongue somewhat in cheek:

- The National Bible Society of Scotland issued an advert in the early part of the century and recently quoted it at their conference:
  Holy Bible, Writ Divine,
     Bound in leather, one pound, nine.
  Satan trembles when he sees,
     Bibles sold as cheap as these.

Should we Friends not know our Bibles better? And speaking of not knowing one's Bible, I remember in 1942 when I was serving in Lisbon, Portugal, with the American Friends Service Committee, we held our very small Meeting for Worship in the office. It happened that Henry Joel Cadbury [1883-1974], Hollis Professor of Divinity at Harvard, one of the translators of *The New English Bible*, and chairman of the American Friends Service Committee, was present with us. I was moved to speak.

- As I think of all the good and evil in the world, the words of the Brahams <u>Requiem</u>, which I sang at Harvard, come to mind. "Behold all flesh is as the grass, and all the goodliness of man is as the flower of grass. For, lo, the grass withereth, but the flower thereof endureth." Oh, may we be strengthened to do the good work that will endure!

At the close of Meeting, I suddenly realized that I had quoted the words wrong. Actually, they should have been "...and the flower thereof decayeth, but the word of the Lord endureth."

I was terribly embarrassed and said so to Henry Cadbury. "Well, Eric," Henry replied, "I thought something didn't sound quite right. But, thee knows, some of the best sermons I have ever heard in Meetings for Worship have been based on misquotations from the Bible."

What encouragement for an ignorant young Friend!

Many Friends tend to look at the Bible very skeptically. The same goes for other religious literature, like hymns. In this connection a Friend said:

- We Quakers don't sing very well, especially hymns. I think the reason is that we are always looking a stanza ahead to see if we agree with it. Perhaps we should suspend disbelief sometimes and sing joyously!

Other Friends sometimes comment on our lack of fire and sparkle:

- This Meeting is like a fire burning with a dull glow because the sticks are damp. [Pause.] What we need is a lot of dry sticks!

This occasional dullness (and please remember, this book is titled *Quaker Meeting: A Risky Business!*) is not new. In 1739, in Chester, Pennsylvania, a number of members were seen to be overcome with drowsiness. A Friend, John Salkeld, sprang to his feet and shouted:

- Fire! Fire! [Everyone was suddenly awake, some asking audibly, "Where?! Where?!] In Hell—to burn up the drowsy and unconcerned.

It is not only in Meeting that Friends get drowsy. John Kimber of Ackworth, Georgia tells this story:

- My mother and her sister, Aunt Marion Emlen, both born in Germantown, were ardent Quakers of many generations. However straight-laced they may have been, things sometimes got out of hand.

    The two families were accustomed to alternating New Year's and Christmas dinners together in each other's homes. At one of these, after an unusually long period of silent grace, Uncle Sam, who was carving a huge roast at the head of the table, noticed that my father, at the foot of that long table, had his chin on his chest and appeared to have fallen asleep. Uncle Sam speared a baked potato with his fork and flipped it toward Father. It made a graceful arc through the air and landed squarely in his coffee cup, which literally exploded. Father jerked upright and said, "Good Lord, I've been torpedoed!"

Amidst the laughter, he turned scarlet and apologized, but the old sailor would never admit that he had been dreaming.

At a recent Meeting in Germantown, a dignified lady, who sat on the facing bench, gave a long message that ended with the question, "What shall we do to be saved?"

A young member, quickly rose and said:

- Swim!

Here's another pleasingly brief message, so thought-provoking that it stimulated a number of interesting responses later in the Meeting.

- What is God for us, a spare tire or a steering wheel?

When my wife and I spent a year, 1985-1986, in England, we attended a very small Meeting in Charlbury, near Oxford. A ten-year-old boy was permitted to bring—or perhaps he insisted on bringing—a pet to Meeting. One Sunday it was a parrot, another Sunday it was a cat. Early in Meeting on one of the parrot Sundays, the bird said loudly:

- Squawk!

Almost at once a Friend said:

- I think we are blessed by the brevity of the message we have just heard.

On a cat Sunday, I was looking at the animal, lying peacefully but alert on the boy's lap, and suddenly I was moved to say:

- I look at our beautiful, peaceful attender, the cat. A most unlikely question has come into my mind: Do cats have souls?

This led to some ministry that was almost theological.

Quakers do not general believe in God's judgement, or even "Acts of God," whether they be in insurance policies or not. But a few years ago in our Germantown Meeting a Friend said:

- When I was about ten years old, I was playing with my friend Stanley Yarnall just outside an open window of our house. My mother called, "It's time for lunch. Come in right now!"

  Stanley and I were having a good time together and didn't want to be interrupted by lunch, so we loudly faked up a fight, with much yelling and pretended hostility, which gave me an excuse to chase Stanley, with fake rage, away from the

house and into a vacant lot across the street. By now, we were so joyously into the fight that when Stanley, smaller and lighter than I was, came to a tulip poplar, he jumped up to grab a small branch, and worked his way up the tree, yelling, "I bet you can't catch me!"

I was challenged. I grabbed the small branch, but as I hoisted myself up, it snapped, and I fell heavily to the ground, stopping my fall with my left arm. I heard a sharp crack, and I felt a sharp pain in my arm. I looked at it. My arm was obviously broken.

I humbly and painfully walked home for lunch and told Mother what had happened. After a visit to the hospital, the setting and splinting of the arm, I spent several days in bed.

I was not a religious kid, but I felt deeply: God did it. God made me fall. It is God's judgment against me for faking a fight—for lying to my mother.

Does God, indeed, judge and punish us for our iniquities?

At another Meeting, a Friend told this story about—metaphorically speaking—God's judgment, or hoped-for judgment:

- A Quaker lady was prudently driving her car when she was crashed into by a reckless, uncaring, unconcerned youth. After they had exchanged license numbers and persuaded some onlookers to act as witnesses, the Quaker said to the youth, in as f(F)riendly a manner as she could manage: "Dear friend, I hope when thee arrives home, they mother comes out from under the porch and bites thee."

  Perhaps this is as near as Friends dare to come to calling someone an SOB and, doubtless, the youth didn't get it.

  What a wonderful example this is of how, in times of crisis, Friends can keep their sense of humor and benignly get rid of their hostility!

Friends, at least in Philadelphia Yearly Meeting, have a mild Query about alcohol and tobacco: "Are you aware of the great waste of human and economic resources resulting from the use of alcohol and tobacco...?" Following the reading of this Query, someone said in Meeting:

- A Friend who smoked died and appeared at the Pearly Gates. He met St. Peter, who looked in his book for his name, but couldn't find it. The recently deceased Friend asked him to look again, which he did, but still no name. This went on several more times and finally St. Peter said, "Oh, Friend, here is thy name; it is almost obscured with tobacco smoke."

And Henry Cadbury, a realist and a non-smoker, said:

- Praise, like smoking, is not harmful unless it is inhaled.

This reminds me of a true story, that took place at Germantown Friends School and was told many years later at Paul McKoy's memorial service.

- One morning the school principal, Mr. Henry Scattergood, came into his office and found a jar of something green in the middle of his desk. A note, in careful, childish handwriting, was attached:

    Dear Mr. Scattergood,

    Our class was making applesauce. Some of it we are giving to Miss Dewsnap [head of the lower school]. Some we are giving to other people we think deserve applesauce. We think you especially deserve some applesauce, and so we are sending you a quart of applesauce.

    > Sincerely yours,
    > Paul McKoy
    > Fifth grade

To return for a moment from praise to smoking, I'll report that Friends enjoy the account of the Devil, presiding over the entrance to Hell (to which, of course, very few Friends go, since they don't believe in that place), who asks each entrant: "Smoking or non-smoking?"

Now on to even nobler subjects. A Friend wrote to me: "The sessions of Philadelphia Yearly Meeting were not going well and someone said jokingly that it might be because the Star Magnolia in the yard, which had traditionally bloomed during Yearly Meeting time, hadn't bloomed that year. But the next morning as people arrived for the day's session, you could hear people saying to each other, 'The magnolia has bloomed!'

"Things went smoothly that day and it wasn't until later that someone discovered that a few of the younger Friends had tied white paper blossoms to the bare branches. Whoever—however—whatever, it had worked!"

And a similar incident happened in England. An elderly woman Friend, speaking with a "rural local accent," and after a terrific gale that had littered the ground with an "awful mess of dead branches and debris from the surrounding trees," said:

- I was appalled at the mess this gale has caused. And then suddenly I saw that the light streams through, as it never did before, giving us a renewed vision of the meaning of life, cleared of its branches.

A Friend afterward commented: "It was a parable of unforgettable simplicity."

And so we come to another area: Who best controls the weather for the benefit of human activity—Jews or Quakers? Here is what one Friend said in Meeting:

- Friends are supposed—or suppose themselves—to be able to speak directly with God, and God directly to them, without the intervention of priests or holy figures. Well, I am a jogger, and I jog with a Jew. Since 1968, we have jogged some 25,000 miles together, and we decided to see which of us was the most powerful in controlling the weather—Eli, who had to work through Moses, or I, the Quaker, who had a direct relationship to God.

You remember, of course, that Moses, on orders from God, was able to have the waters of the Red Sea part, and so the Jews escaped from slavery and the pursuing troops of the Pharaoh were swallowed up by the returning flood. Pretty powerful!

So Eli and I kept an informal record, and it turned out that Eli, working through Moses, was much more effective in turning off the rain (or snow) than I was, despite my direct pipeline to the Almighty. When I jogged alone, I got rained on; when Eli jogged alone, he didn't. When we jogged together, Eli's power-through-Moses worked, and it was dry—not 100 percent, but there was a statistically significant difference.

We affectionately called our experience "the Red Sea Syndrome."

So, Friends, we must be modest in our claims to have a direct pipeline to God.

Needless to say, this ministry aroused some response both in Meeting and in Friend-to-Friend conversation over several months. A report of it even got published in *The Philadelphia Inquirer*.

Sometimes Friends are very, very careful about what they say in Meeting. The husband of such a Friend reported to me:

- The first time one speaks in Meeting is often memorable—at least to the one who speaks,

    As a teacher, in Germantown Friends School Thursday Meetings, and a regular First Day attender, Jayne Wilhelm had great respect for the silence of Meeting. I think she spoke in Meeting only once in four decades of being a staunch Quaker.

    Yet, in a family dinner table discussion of spiritual growth, she told us, "I spoke in Meeting once, about nine years ago, but lately I've wondered if I ought not stand up and tell everybody that what I meant to say was . . ."

Such glorious caution! And it may even seem to you as peculiar, but then Quakers have long classified themselves as "a peculiar people," not like others. There is a famous story about this classification. It was told by Rufus Jones, but also by many others, including deeply loving married couples to each other. The story goes thus: One winter's evening, a Quaker farmer and his wife were sitting in front of the fire having a long argument. He serenely smoked his pipe while she knitted a sweater more and more furiously as the evening and argument wore on. Finally, in desperation, she dropped her knitting and, turning toward him, said, "Husband, everybody's queer but me and thee. And sometimes I think thee's a bit queer!"

Well, let's close this chapter on comical and humorous messages by a report of a Meeting for Worship which took place recently on a gorgeous spring day in April. The first speaker, an avid and expert photographer, exclaimed about the beauties of spring, and how an eight-hour botanical trip the day before through the Susquehanna Valley had combined the admiration of nature's beauty with a deep sense of worship.

The next speaker, who very seldom speaks, arose and said:

- "God's in his heaven,
  All's right with the world!"
    How strongly I feel this today. I haven't thought of that poem for some fifty-two years. As I remember, the poet says, "The snail's on the wing, the lark's on the ???" Hmm? Where is the snail, anyway? Anyway, all's right with the world and God is in his heaven!*

Speakers who followed said that all is *not* right with the world. Consider the poor and the suffering; and: It's what we *do*, upheld by God, that can make all right with the world.

Finally Meeting was closed with the traditional shaking of hands, and the closer, before making announcements, said: "This has been an extraordinary Meeting! I shall never be able to get out of my mind the wonderful image: 'The snail's on the wing.' How uplifting!"

---

*The speaker was trying to quote the poem *Pippa Passes: Morning*, by Robert Browning (1812-89):

The year's at the spring
And day's at the morn;
Morning's at seven;
The hill-side's dew-pearled;
The lark's on the wing;
The snail's on the thorn;
God's in his heaven —
All's right with the world!

Chapter VI: Children in Meeting—Something Special

Children are marvelous beings to have in Meeting, even though they can cause troubles as well as delights. Nowadays most Meetings arrange to provide child care for the little ones and sometimes special sessions for young adolescents. In some Meetings the children stay in Meeting for the first ten to fifteen minutes and then go out to child care; in others the youngsters come in for the last ten to fifteen minutes.

Children's Messages—Intentional and Unintentional

I have already told of the reaction to a very little child's "Bye-bye" ("God be with you") message. Here are a few other "messages," or accounts of messages:

- An aunt named Rennie was taking a young niece and nephew to Meeting one Sunday. On the way, mischievous Becky, about twelve, whispered to Steve, about seven, "Aunt Rennie will give you a dime if you say something in Meeting."

  As Meeting progressed, Steve stood up and delivered a very mature message for a seven-year-old. Aunt Rennie, who knew nothing of the conspiracy, was astounded and proud, showing these emotions on her face.

  When he sat down, Steve turned to his aunt, and in a very audible whisper asked, "Do I get the dime now?"

- A Friend tells of sitting in a Meeting held especially for younger members, with his four-year-old son on his lap. After several others had risen to speak, the boy apparently felt a leading also. He stood and said, "God is..." then trailed off. A moment later he tried again: "God is..." and lapsed again into silence, this time until the end of Meeting. He then whispered in his father's ear, "Dad, I'm sorry I don't know what God is, but I'm really going to try and find out."

This four-year-old didn't know what God is, but some four-to-six-year olds have a pretty good variety of ideas on the subject. At a pre-primary class held for two months at Germantown Meeting, the children held a short Meeting for Worship early in their hour together. At one of the Meetings, they started talking about God. Here, recorded afterwards by the teacher, are some of the thoughts they had.

- God is all around you. He's even inside you. Sometimes he's in your head and sometimes he's in your heart....God is even with dead people. He's inside everybody and everything....God is both a boy and a girl—he's both....He's a spirit.... God is like a bird....God is like a candle inside you and it's like when you put your finger quickly back and forth through the candle flame—it jumps on you, but doesn't burn you—it's warm and doesn't hurt....God creates everything. Sometimes he talks to you—he doesn't really talk, you just feel the talking inside you....Sometimes God doesn't let you do the things you want to do. He has a little ball with all the colors of the outside world and we live inside it....We are quiet in Meeting to listen for God to hear what we are supposed to do and when you are supposed to speak....We go to Quaker Meeting to talk about God.

- A young child attending Meeting for the first time, after a rather long period of silence asked his mother in a voice quite audible to all, "Mommy, why is everybody so quiet?" He received a whispered answer directly in his ear.

  After a few moments a Friend on the facing bench arose and stated, **"The first speaker has raised a most important question...."**

- One of the most moving Meetings I've attended was one where a five-year-old stood and was clearly about to speak. His father leaned over to grab him, but the boy dodged his grab and delivered a most passionate and tenderly grieving message about how sad he felt that the dinosaurs were extinct. He spoke for several minutes and when he sat down there was a rich silence.

Then an adult stood and talked about the importance of caring for all God's creatures. The whole Meeting that followed was on the theme of stewardship.

- A high school teacher who had attended Meeting for Worship regularly for a considerable length of time rose one day to speak about how meaningful the previous Meeting had been.

  Slowly she pictured how a three- or four-year-old child had left her mother's side, walked slowly to the Sunday School part of the Meetinghouse, thumbing the books, putting her fingers into the unlit stove (it was summer), and passing her hands lovingly over the melodian in the room. Then, quietly, she had climbed the steps to the clerk's desk and stood there a while, smiling as she swung her feet back and forth.

  "I am a strict disciplinarian," commented the speaker. "But I was impressed with how the Meeting for Worship was not disturbed by behavior of this child and, in fact, seemed to weave her activities into their worship." She concluded, "That was the best Meeting for Worship I have experienced in my many times here."

Children's Reactions to Messages

Young Friends do not always understand—at least in an adult way—messages given in Meeting.

- A father and his small son were listening to a speaker who in the course of his message, quoted impressively from the scriptures: "Be still and know that I am God." [Psalm 46,10] He paused, and the little boy whispered to his father, "Is he, Daddy?"

Here are two other reactions to stillness, or rather the lack of it:

- A little girl was taken to Meeting for the first time, and her parents impressed on her the importance of being quiet and sitting in silence. After a time a Friend rose and stared to speak. The girl turned to her mother and exclaimed, "Oh, that naughty man!"

- Stephen G. Cary, a weighty and humorous Friend, who has served throughout the world with the American Friends Service Committee, of which he became chairperson of the Board, recalls when he first was allowed to attend Germantown Meeting at about age four. He had begged to go, and finally permission was given after he solemnly promised his mother that he would sit absolutely still for the whole hour.

  All went well for about ten minutes, and then an impressive white-bearded Friend arose and preached. He quoted a passage from the Bible and then paused, at which point young Steve turned to his mother and in a strong, protesting voice said, "Well, if that man can speak, why can't I?"

- Mary Hoxie Jones, the daughter of internationally-known Rufus M. Jones [1863-1948], recalls a time in the Quaker Meeting in South China, Maine: "Father was talking about faith, and he quoted the familiar phrase: 'Faith is the victory.' The minute the Meeting was over two young children rushed up to him, breathless with excitement. "Cousin Rufus, you were talking about *us!*" "So I was," he replied enthusiastically. "Of course I was!" he added when he recognized his small audience. The children were Faith Jones and Victor Stimpson.

More Reactions to Meetings for Worship, Spiritual and Otherwise

- A family had been going to Meeting for a few months, and one Sunday on the way home, Heidi, age six, said, "When people speak in Meeting, I think angels take the messages and put them on God's bulletin board."

- At High Bentham Meeting in England, there is an easily-visible clock on the wall. The Meeting was, in a manner, presided over by two leading men Friends, Townley and Baldwin, who always sat next to each other, facing the Meeting. Townley strongly believed that Meeting should finish with a prayer; Baldwin was a stickler for punctuality.

    We younger members of the Meeting used to run a competition as to whether Old Man Townley would manage to sink to his knees or would have his hand gripped in a firm handshake first. It used to be a very near thing—and we would keep careful score.

- There is an expression used by Friends: that Meeting is ended "by the shaking of hands." Children are often puzzled by how the closers of Meeting know when to shake hands or whether they themselves might terminate the worship by holding their hands up in the air and shaking them. I once tried this when I was a boy, but it didn't work and my mother laughingly reprimanded me afterwards so that I never tried again.

    Also, years ago, in order to ensure punctual closing (even though in Friends' theory, Meeting should be closed when the spirit indicates), there was a small, carefully-crafted wooden box behind the railing of the facing benches where no one but the Meeting closer could see it. In this box the caretaker of the Meeting hung on a small nail a gold watch, wound and carefully set. I remember being a bit disillusioned when I first saw it and realized that not God but a machine said when to end Meeting. Also, it seemed a bit hypocritical to pretend, by hiding it, that there was no secular timepiece.

- Children remember vividly certain non-verbal noises in Meeting. A number of years ago, when audio-technology was less advanced than it is today, whenever someone rose and began to speak, there was immediately the sound of hearing aids being turned up so high that they squeaked. A kid I knew told me it was God objecting to the "braking" of the silence. And a Friend, Jim Baldwin, remembers his first audible introduction to Meeting: it was a slow rhythmic squeak made by the leather belt of an older woman as she breathed in and out.

- One small child at her first Meeting for Worship, when asked afterward what her reaction was, said, "I thought it was terrible—enough to drive the Devil himself away." On the other hand, when children become accustomed to Meeting, often they grow to like it. Thus when Tim Nicholson was taken by his parents to a Methodist church during a vacation in Ocean City, New Jersey, as the Order of Service rolled along, he leaned over to his mother and whispered, "When do they give you time to think?" (Tim Nicholson later became a prominent Friend and clerk of the large Friends Meeting in Cambridge, Massachusetts.)

- Yes, in Meeting children do have time to think. After Meeting for Worship at Haverford, Pennsylvania, Lois Kelly, the daughter of Thomas and Lael Kelly, told her mother that she had been thinking in Meeting about whom she loved best. Anxious to encourage her daughter, Lael commented, "Now that was a very good idea. And what was your decision?"

  Lois replied, "I decided I loved Daddy best, then, God, and then Rufus Jones and Henry Bartlett"—all of whom she knew and sat on the facing benches.

  Apparently Lois knew that God had to come in somewhere in her list—but not ahead of her father whom she could know directly.

Some Children's Mischief and Troubles in Meeting

It's not surprising that children make trouble—most of it minor—Meeting for Worship. After all, silent waiting and wriggly vigor are somewhat uncongenial. Here are a few examples of the stories people have told me about or I have experienced.

- A ten-year-old boy played a prank on his mother who possessed a rather unQuakerly crowning glory of long red hair which she held in place with tortoise shell hairpins. When the boy noticed that his mother's eyes were closed and that she probably had fallen asleep, he very quietly and gently removed the hairpins so that suddenly the auburn tresses fell all around her shoulders. She suddenly awoke in a terrible state of embarrassment and dishabille. Her son pretended to be in deep, silent contemplation.

- Stephen Cary, the now-weighty Friend whom I have already mentioned, knew as a boy that the floor of Germantown Meeting (a very large room) slanted gently from back to front. He kept a marble or two in the cuff of his trousers and, when the silence was deep, would place the marble on the floor so that it rolled slowly and audibly from where he sat to the front. It was, to say the least, disturbing to worship.

- Another boy was fiddling with a ring on his finger when it suddenly came off, fell into the heading register, and loudly rolled down to the furnace. Reports the boy, now an experienced weighty Friend, "I was sure that everyone was looking at me, so for the rest of Meeting I was somewhat better behaved."

- Sometimes things larger and more complicated fall on the Meetinghouse floor. In Charlbury Meeting, Oxfordshire, in about 1938, there was a sudden loud bump, and a little boy sitting next to his mother, having fallen asleep, slipped onto the floor. His mother looked down at him, put out her foot, flattened him suitably, and he continued to sleep while the Meeting continued undisturbed.

- The above-mentioned Stephen Cary and his friend Larry Kimber were about fourteen years old and attending Meeting in Jamestown, Rhode Island. It was summer, the windows were open, and the Meetinghouse was right in the middle of a meadow in which were some cows and calves. During Meeting, a cow and a calf began a loud and clear dialogue: "mooooo" (deep); "mooooo" (high). It was clearly a meaningful communication, but humorous to two young adolescent nonbovines. Steve and Larry began to laugh. In fact, they were so convulsed that the bench shook and they had to be separated. From then till the end of Meeting they periodically and silently shook the benches with laughter.

- Nathan was about three years old when he leaned over during Meeting for Worship and bit his baby brother's toe to make him cry. Then, in a loud, clear voice, he said, **"Be quiet, Aaron, or you'll wake the people up."**

Ways to Keep Children Out of Trouble in Meeting— Mostly Discovered by the Kids Themselves

You have now read examples of trouble-making instead of worship. How about mischief-prevention?

- My parents wanted to be sure that their children were thoroughly indoctrinated into Quakerism. One of their methods was to require that we attend Meeting each Sunday as soon as they judged that we could sit quietly for an hour without too much squirming. Mother was always careful to separate my brother Don and me. Nevertheless we shared many ways of assuaging our boredom, including the counting from our bench of the number of verticle slats that made up the wainscoting that ran on the wall behind the facing benches. I recall the number as 192, but our count would vary week by week by as much as four or five thus giving us our first lesson in standard mean deviation.

- Another technique involving counting was to count the syllables in the words of well-known songs and compare notes after Meeting.

- A middle-aged Friend reports to me: "You are a featured actor as I consider not so much humor in Meeting, but levity in the sense of lightening or lifting. The best example is when you spoke of how, as a small boy, you contemplated the Germantown Meeting room as a wonderful place to set up electric trains. The long, straight aisles—great for speeding, the curves under the tunnel-like benches—great for invention of patterns. After you spoke, I am sure most of us, adult or child, found that room much friendlier (emphatically small 'f') and more interesting."

- Another Friend, now many times a grandmother, and the widow of an American Friends Service Committee worker killed in a plane crash over Iceland while en route to Europe: "I often played with my father's big gold pocket watch. This day he leaned down whispering, 'Try to sit still by counting all the things thee's grateful for.' For the rest of Meeting I sat very straight, putting my father's watch back in his vest pocket.

I counted—but I think it was that day I learned to sit quietly in Meeting and not put my head down in Daddy's lap. I was grown-up now. I was eight years old and had a baby brother.

- The same Friend reports: "My grandfather sat on the very last bench, and we could often turn and look at each other. His blue, squinty, sea captain's eyes behind a pince-nez were kind. He would wink at me and tweak his black bow tie which he wore with a stiff white collar. I wore a little black ribbon bow at the collar of my guimpe or shirtwaist which was worn under a jumper dress. Our bow-ties were like a shared secret, and he always smiled when I wore mine."

- A less decent but I'm sure perfectly innocent pastime, according to another Friend, was to imagine—in detail—what the older members of Meeting would look like if they wore no clothes.

- Parents over the years tried to figure the best sort of things to give little children to fiddle with during Meeting. For a time, as I remember, rubber bands were considered quite good, until the kids stretched them a bit carelessly and they would spring loose and fly through the air, disturbing worship. But one parent thought up the perfect fiddle things: pipe cleaners — bendable, shapable, soft, unspringing, and always totally silent. (This idea was even reported to Monthly Meeting for Business [see Chapter 8] when Friends were weightily discussing how to improve the quality of worship.)

- I can remember vividly an occasion which made me, at age eight suddenly determine to behave better in Meeting. I was getting restless one Sunday and decided to lie down on the bench. My parents ignored this, but I as I lay I turned my head sideways so that I could see the bench behind, and there sat—unsmiling, even severe looking—my third grade teacher, Miss Mendenhall. My heart leapt with terror, I sat up straight, and was perfectly still for several Meetings to come. I remember that, for a moment, Miss Mendenhall's eyes seemed like those of an all-seeing, strict God—God looking at bad little me.

-oOo-

These methods and many others generally work pretty well. A young girl, Heidi, age six, was visiting her grandmother's Congregational Church. Of course, there was something happening all the time as the Sunday service proceeded. After the service, and elderly woman sitting behind her said, "Heidi, you were so quiet during that long service!"

Heidi replied, "I'm always quiet. I'm a Quaker."

Chapter VII: Meetings for Worship in Friends' Schools

You might think that Friends Meetings held under the auspices of a well-disciplined school filled with intelligent students and with teachers and administrators participating would not be "a risky business." Well, think again and read on.

Meeting at Friends Select School, Philadelphia.   *Photo credit: Rosemary Ranck*

All Friends' schools, and a few Friends' colleges,* require their students, even the youngest ones, to attend Meeting for Worship each week, usually on Thursdays. The purpose of this requirement is not to try to convert the students to membership in the Society of Friends—to "convince" them—but to give them a religious experience in the broadest sense of the term.

It may seem strange for Friends schools to do this, especially since only about 5 to 25 percent of their students are Quakers—in most Friends' schools there are many more Jewish than Quaker students enrolled (and also Catholics, Methodists, Amish, Episcopalians, Muslims, born-again Christians, agnostics, and atheists), but there is no doubt that the experience of Meeting is very meaningful to most students. When surveys of alumni are made about the strengths and weaknesses of the schools, many, many graduates, often years later, volunteer the opinion that Meeting for Worship was them most meaningful and valuable experience of their school years, even though on any given Thursday, a given alum probably would have chosen not to attend had he or she been given the choice. Here are some typical comments:

- Meeting for Worship was at the heart of my twelve years at Germantown Friends School. [Class of 1950]

- I have come to feel a strong love of Quaker Meeting and a bond to it. I do not feel that this conflicts with my Jewish background, or my unsureness about the existence of God. I missed Meeting during my first year at college and found that I needed to make time to be alone and think. Meeting would come wonderfully back to me at strange times. [Class of 1987]

- It is hard enough now, as it was in my day, to set young people straight on matters of behavior and deeper moral questions of what is important in life. Although I often didn't want to go to Meeting, now I know that it was vital to the captive Meeting audience. [Class of 1927]

- I often hated Meeting—a few times, I cheated and hid in a little room hoping that no one would find me or notice that I was absent—but now I realize that I'm a deeper, better person, more strongly striving for a better world, because I was required to be in Meeting on Thursdays. [Class of 1968]

Also, in many Friends' schools, it has become a sort of unplanned student-initiated practice at the last Meeting of the year for the Seniors, and sometimes others, to speak in nostalgic, sentimental, sometimes almost maudlin terms about their school, their friends, their appreciation for all that they have experienced, and especially about the meaningfulness of Meeting for Worship. At Moorestown Friends School, in New Jersey, one Senior spoke of how much the secretary of the

---

*Friends' colleges do provide a weekly Meeting for Worship with attendance optional, and a very small proportion of the students actually attend Meeting.

School had meant to her, and then she got up from her seat, went quickly over to the secretary, and hugged her. There were tears of joy and sentiment throughout the Meetinghouse.

-oOo-

In large Friends' schools that go from kindergarten through twelfth grade, there are separate lower school (K-6) and upper school (7-12) Meetings for Worship. And, at whatever level, they can be "a risky business," because they are unprogrammed, just as regular Sunday Meetings are. The risks—delights, wonders, outrages, and inspirations—tend to be somewhat different, depending upon the age of the attenders.

Meetings in Elementary School

Let's start at the earliest age, kindergarten. A teacher at West Chester (Pennsylvania) Friends School writes that each "PrePrimary" child was accompanied to Meeting for Worship by a third- or fourth-grader. After returning from their first Meeting, according to their teacher, Bunny DeCray, the children commented:

"It was quiet."
"I liked it when the person talked about sharing."
"I liked my partner, who was in the fourth grade."
"I liked Teacher Alta's poem."
"I liked it when I saw my brother."
"It made me have a good feeling to be with everyone."
"All the people that were around us felt like a whole family."
"I liked it; it was nice."
"I liked it because it was quiet, and I like to think about God."

- In a K-6 Meeting, a *kindergartner* stood and said: "The Meetinghouse just turned upside down in my mind. Then it sort of came back into place. It was queer! Everything now has a new look."

  Teacher: "Yes, our minds can flip things. While you sit here, try flipping your mind two years forward and then two years backward. What do you see in your life?"

  Several children, each after a very brief moment of silence: "My father told me how to get along with people in a new way. I'm trying it out and it's working." ... "I flip my mind into my older brother's mind. Usually I don't like the way he acts, but when I flip into his mind, I like him better." ... "I fell down and hurt my elbow on the pavement. All day after that my mind was in my elbow, and I couldn't think." ... "It's easier to flip a coin than to flip a mind. And with a coin there are only two ways it can come up, heads or tails. But with our minds in our heads things can come up in a lot of different ways. I think we should keep flipping."

Teacher: "This morning, I woke up late. I rushed to get off to school, but I couldn't find my keys. My mind started flipping into worries: Who will let my first and second graders into our room? What will they do? I called the school switch- board but no one answered. Suddenly I found my keys under a sweater. I rushed off to school, all worried, but when I got there, I found that someone had opened my room and let them in, and they were all happily busy at their projects. Suddenly, I saw life in a good new way, and my day turned around. It flipped."

- At a Thanksgiving lower school Meeting at Abington (Pennsylvania) Friends School, the principal gave a brief message about the holiday and closed with the question, **"And what have you to be thankful for?"**
  A long, deep period of silence followed. Then a small boy whose legs dangled from the front row Meetinghouse bench stood up and said with the assurance of an experienced preacher, **"Christmas!!"** and sat down.

Before we go on to further reports of Meetings for Worship, I should make it clear that there are two ways that school Meetings can go wrong. One is the "popcorn Meeting," most common in elementary school, in which children pop up one after another and say a brief sentence or two and sit down. None of the utterances seems to have any relation to those that preceded it. The second way, most common in upper school Meetings, is for the Meeting to turn into a debate on a subject, quite different from worship. (See page 78 for a prime example, in which a student rose and began, "Well, getting back to the subject....") But *let's* get back to the subject, elementary school Meetings for Worship.

- The only message: "When I was little at my grandmother's house, I was playing beside a bookcase. Suddenly, I don't remember why, all the books fell out and not one hit me. My mother came in and said it was as if God's hand reached out and covered my head so that I didn't get hurt."

- Mostly kindergartners: "When I get home, I like to play with my kitty cat. It is cute and soft and funny to play with. This is a nice way to come home." ... "We had two cats, one white, one three colors. We finally had to give them away because they were going to the bathroom all over the place. My mother said they were outside cats, not inside." ... "We have a dog. One day it couldn't walk. My dad put him in the car and took him to the vet. When we got there, the dog hopped out of the car and walked! We don't know what was the matter with him or how he cured himself. Neither did the vet." ... "I had a dog and we had to give it away. It made me sad" ... "Pets can make you sad and pets can make you glad. So can people."

- *Girl:* "It was my mother's birthday and we were watching a Walt Disney movie. We heard an awful bang. We went upstairs, and there was a house burning. Three people died and a car blew up." ... *Boy:* "I was alone in the kindergarten. I played with the blocks in the blocks corner. I play that way here in Meeting." ... *Girl:* "I think Kate's story was scary. Sometimes it's lightning that makes houses burn. It's scary to have fire or lightning. I can see why Kate was scared." ... *Boy:* "I used to go to Miquon [an excellent nearby elementary school]. My parents told me I had to come to GFS [Germantown Friends School]. I didn't want to; I hated the idea. I guess I was scared to change. Now I've been here a while and time has passed so quickly and I like it. Sometimes things you hate to do and think are going to be awful turn out well."

- *Kindergartner Phoebe:* "Two girls in our class ran away. They played in a tent in somebody's yard. The police brought them back. Mrs. Workman [the kindergarten teacher] said we must never run away. There is a lot of danger out there. It worries everyone. If you are going anywhere, you must tell someone so they won't worry and know where you are all the time." ... *Kindergartner:* "Missy and Kate ran away. The whole kindergarten went into Mr. Harkin's [lower school principal] office with the policeman and Mrs. Workman. Running away is a dangerous thing." ... *Teacher:* "Running away was in my mind even before Phoebe spoke. My class has just written stories about why people run away—why do they run away? Where do they run to? What do they find scary? But I've been thinking about some plants I have planted. They cannot move. They can <u>adapt,</u> usually, to too little water or too much, but they cannot move. Also, many of the people in Russia around Chernobyl, where the atomic energy plant blew up, tried to run away. The place was poisoned. But most of them had no place to go and had to stay. Most of <u>us</u> cannot move. We stay put; we adapt.

- *Child:* "We should have good manners. We should try to be nice to people even if we don't want to or it's hard and we'd rather be nasty." ... *Music teacher:* "It's interesting how in Meeting one thinks about something that others are thinking about, too. Yesterday afternoon, a group of us were talking about manners, not only the 'thank you' and 'please' kind, but showing respect and concern for others. Last evening here in the Meetinghouse a lack of manners was shown by people talking and not paying attention to what the leader wanted." .... *Child:* "Manners—I mean showing care for one another—is the most important lesson to learn in school." ... *Teacher:* "Getting along, sharing politeness, can be only surface—because 'Mother said so!' But real manners come from inside. They are the outward sign of caring and thoughtfulness."

- *An older member of Meeting:* "At a recent Meeting for Business of our Monthly Meeting, someone who had to give a report had laryngitis. He had to whisper. Everyone strained to hear. It was amazing: people seemed to learn more that way. And we all need to learn to listen more carefully." ... *Lower School Principal:* "Where I used to teach, everyone had to yell at people. But, just as our Friend has said, a teacher came in one day with laryngitis, and the class behaved better, were very attentive. So the teacher stretched out her laryngitis as long as she could. So remember: We need changes in voice levels to remind us to listen, to really listen and hear what people are saying."

- *Teacher:* "You all have heard the saying, 'Great oaks from little acorns grow.' But think of it! An acorn no bigger than this [a gesture]; it can become an oak much higher than this Meetinghouse. It is the same way with the little things we all are learning at this school about friendship and life." ... *Fifth-grade boy:* "It's true about friends, and how we can keep them and make them grow. So this summer I am going to work on friendship, even with people I don't like."

- *Teacher:* "It is very hard to learn to cooperate—to work with other people smoothly and exactly. Learning how to row a boat with seven other oarsmen is hard. And in some ways it is like learning to sit in Meeting. Each of us has to learn to pull his oar and learn to sit alone—together—and listen to each other, to the voice of the spirit, to God."

- *Older member of Meeting:* "When I jog in our neighborhood at about the time the local middle school is dismissed, I hear yells of joy at escaping from the school, but when I see the students a few minutes later along the path, they look so glum and sad, as if there were no joy in learning or in their lives, so different from you!" ... *Teacher:* "There is a very cheerful, friendly boy now in the upper school, who has always been that way. He is always full of positive thoughts and offers to help. Just seeing him always makes me feel stronger and better. How I would love it if I am remembered that way by the people I teach!"

- *Older member of Meeting:* "Cooperation—working together—sometimes can mean the difference between getting there or not. I think of an example of two of our upper school students who were paddling from southern Canada to Hudson Bay. It became a long, tiring trip, and as they found themselves pressed for time, they became irritable and began to fight and quarrel over every problem and every discussion. They almost resorted to fisticuffs—to hitting each other. Then suddenly they both realized that if they worked together they could make it, but if they worked apart or against each other, they could not. They made it! ..." *Child:* "Even when your parents scold you, they still love you." ... *Child:* "It's the fun of playing the game that counts, not just winning. God makes you a winner anyway." ... *Member of Meeting:* "Many ideas are floating around in this room. As we settle in, we all fit into a pattern. Can you find a pattern?"

- *Teacher:* "Think about wolves in stories you know. Do they represent evil?—Little Red Ridinghood? Three Little Pigs? Never Cry Wolf. All the evil characters seem to be fat. I have been fat. It is very hard in life when you are fat—you are teased; people won't play with you, they shut you out. But if you are fat, or some other way that people don't like, it makes you more understanding about prejudice." ... *Child:* "I don't care if you're fat or skinny, or white or black, or bright or dull, or pretty or ugly, or Jewish or Quaker, or dog or cat, or anything, I look underneath and I try to love you."

Meetings in Upper School

The lower school Meetings you have just read about could be reported because one teacher made careful notes just after Meeting as an unofficial record for the school. I don't know of anyone who has made such notes for upper schools, except occasionally. Here, though, are some accounts of various bits that people have sent me.

Messages that Stimulated All Worshipers

- *Senior girl:* "I have a friend who has AIDS. When he told me, I embraced him with a deep love. Later, I was amazed at my reaction. I would have expected it to be revulsion."

- *Eighth-grade boy:* "We've just had Halloween. We all wore masks. But in real life, today, here, we all wear masks. Maybe it's time to take them off."

- *Report to me from a parent:* "Our two sons are graduates of the William Penn Charter School. In the spring of 1981, our eldest obviously was overcome with a combination of Spring Fever and 'Senioritis' because he stood up at the last Meeting of the school term and made the following pronouncement: 'I would like to quote the words of two individuals who have had the profoundest effect upon me during my years at Penn Charter.' First: 'Obviously, I am surrounded by inferior mentalities.' Second: 'It takes a tough man to make a tender chicken.'
   "We learned about this because our son was late arriving home from school this particular day and, when asked the reason why, confessed that the Headmaster had asked him to stop by his office after classes."

- *A tenth grader:* "Some of you know how much I love to play basketball. A few days ago I fell and terribly damaged my elbow. I had to have very complicated surgery. I don't know if I'll ever be able to play again. The thing I love best..." and here the boy broke down and wept. The whole roomful of students united with him, and there were sounds and motions of weeping. No one seemed to be embarrassed or self-conscious. A feeling of love and tenderness filled the room.

- *A teacher:* "Recently I visited a Roman Catholic parochial school. My visit was one of several to many different kinds of schools to survey the attitudes and questions children in grades four through six had about questions concerning love and sex and families. Before I began my survey in the Catholic school, the Sister who was Head took me around to each classroom to introduce me to the students. As soon as we entered each room, the students stood up and faced the Sister and me. When she said, 'Children, this is Mr. Johnson,' they immediately replied, almost in unison, 'God bless you, Mr. Johnson.' I found it an uplifting experience of the power of well-learned good manners."

Memorable Bits in School Meetings

Many people have sent me accounts of single messages in Meeting for Worship that impressed them and have inspired or amused them over the years.

- *An upper school English teacher:* "I have had an Apocryphal Dream. In my dream I am standing in a room very like this one. I am the only one standing and the room is full of people. All of the faces are strange to me and I know none of them. I bow my head, and it occurs to me that I will teach some of the people in the room. I raise my head with some difficulty and a few of the faces are familiar to me. I lowered my head a second time and it occurs to me that some of the people here will teach _me_. It is harder to raise my head this time, but when I do, a few more faces are known to me. On bowing my head a third time, I realize that I will come to care for _all_ of the people in the room. This time it is very difficult to raise my head. But when I do, I know all the faces in the room."

- *A Latin teacher and advisor to an eighth-grade homeroom:* "Many of you know the Beatitudes, the eight blessings, spoken by Jesus at the beginning of the Sermon on the Mount [Matthew 5, 3-12]. Today a new Beatitude has come to me: 'Blessed are those who have to continue to love, for they shall know grief. And through grief they partake of creation.'"

- A *math teacher of many years* who spoke this "message" more than once:
  "A wise old owl sat in our oak;
  The more he heard, the less he spoke;
  The less he spoke the more he heard.
  Why aren't we all like this wise old bird?"

- *The same math teacher:* "Today you are the sum of all your yesterdays. Tomorrow, today will be yesterday. Build well today. You can never erase from the You who is You any act or thought. Each act takes its place as an integral part of your personality the instant it is finished. This law is as unchangeable as the law of the Medes and Persians. It is Nature's law."

- *An English teacher:* "I remember years ago in this very Meetinghouse, an old man with white hair and a red face spoke to us students at great length. At the end he said, in a strong, loud voice, 'If there is one thing you should remember from all I have said today, it is this'—and he raised his arm above his head and extended his forefinger. Well, I'll never forget the words I've just reported to you, but I have no memory of what 'this' was. So, as you go through life, don't expect to be remembered for what _you_ think is important!"

Some Events During Meeting for Worship

Sometimes, more or less related to the silence and the spoken ministry, but sometimes not at all related, events occur which we remember over the years. Here are eight:

- On a warm day, with the doors open, Meeting was just settling down into quiet. Suddenly, stealthily, a large cat entered a side door and walked along the aisle. A teacher stood, reached down for the cat, picked it up and held it high, and carried it out of the Meetinghouse. As he did, a wave of chuckles spread over the whole Meeting, grew louder, then softer, and the Meeting resettled into silence. During the rest of the unprogrammed Meeting, several people spoke about the importance and meaning of humor—humor as a gift of God.

- Sometimes the event begins within the Meeting. A Friends school graduate reports: "There we were, faculty and students, all sitting very quietly, each one off into his own thoughts. All of a sudden, one of the younger students broke the silence with a sneeze. It wasn't just an ordinary sneeze, but colorful and dramatic. It started with an explosive 'A-' and then went into a long, high-pitched 'choo!' which slowly glissandoed down to a lower pitch and then died away, kind of like a feather that gets blown up into the air and then falls slowly back down to the ground. There was silence for a moment, and then *everybody* burst out laughing. So much for the rest of that Meeting."

- Another graduate: "I can recall clearly a Thursday morning Meeting at Germantown Friends School, which occurred during the prime of my class's 7th grade adolescent social groping. One of my classmates who, following a period of perhaps twenty or thirty minutes of completely silent worship, rose to speak, yet stood quietly unable to find words. He remained on his feet, for what seemed an extraordinarily long time, perhaps a full minute, and then sat down. His expression on sitting down was, and remained, strangely puzzled.

  "Following meeting, he was approached by a number of us who were curious about his rising and not saying anything. He replied that he had felt he had to stand, but, although he said he tried, was unable to speak and didn't understand why. He was hardly a silent fellow, most of the time. I never was able to sort out whether he was simply trying to draw attention to himself at the time, or as I think more likely, may have actually felt he should rise and then was either unable or, on second thought, unwilling to share with those in the Meeting."

- In my day [Class of 1936], we entered Meeting in a well-organized fashion. This was my first Meeting for Worship. We seventh-graders led the procession down the fire tower stairs and across the yard to the Meetinghouse. Remember, I for one, and I suspect there were others, had never been in the Meetinghouse before. We were seated way down front, and didn't dare look around to see the rest of the school file in. We sat in silence and waited for things to begin. At least in the Presbyterian church the music changed a bit when it was time to get going. There weren't even any hymn books to look at. The facing bench was imposing, and I am sure that Master Stanley Yarnall was the only really familiar face. The silence was terrible. Then someone on the facing bench rose and spoke, the subject matter has long been forgotten. However, one small classmate (<u>not me</u>) started to applaud when the Friend sat down. A few claps were enough; then he realized that perhaps that was not in order. I had sense enough to play a waiting game to see what others did, but our classmate had a rough time the rest of the Meeting, imagining probably that Master Stanley was staring at him. When the Meeting broke, I do remember trying to get out as fast as I could.

- At one Friends' school, occasionally two students are assigned the function of closing Meeting by shaking hands. A couple of seniors hatched a foul plot and decided they would not "close Meeting" at all, but let it run on and on—never mind the schedule of classes and the rest of the academic day. The silence became intolerable, people began clearing their throats, etc., etc., until, at last, a teacher strode to the facing benches and shook hands with one of the assigned students. (The exit from the Meetinghouse was perhaps the fastest on record.)

- A British Friend reports. The names in his report are those of well-known Friends' schools: "When my brother was at school at Bootham, and the big Meetinghouse in York was thronged with pupils from the two schools, Bootham and the Mount, a man, not a member of the inner circle of Friends, who had spoken in some way unacceptably the week before and been dealt with by the Elders, got up, strode to the front of the Meeting and said: 'I have enemies in this meeting.' Then turning and pointing to each Elder in turn, he went on: 'They are, you, you, and you.' I am afraid I can't say how the episode finished!"

- This from a graduate of Friends' Central School, Philadelphia, of which Barclay Jones was the Principal: "One year (in 1938 or 1939, I don't remember) the senior girls, who sat in the front rows on the right side, after a suitable time of silence, suddenly all crossed their legs the same way at the same time. After a few moments they all recrossed their leg—the same way at the same time. The rest of us, who had known this was to happen, were transfixed with suppressed delight, and all kept our eyes glued on the facing bench. Barclay Jones was not a mirthful man, but, sure enough, a faint smile creased his lips; whoever else was there then laughed!"

- At Haverford College, in the days when attendance at Thursday Meeting was compulsory—and much resented by many students, word got to President Gilbert F. White that a number of students had arranged a betting pool, with suitable odds and expertise, and a fair amount of money at stake. The betting, which is entirely contrary to Quaker principles, was on which of several weighty and excellent Friends would speak in Meeting, and which would speak first.

    President White, with his tongue only half in his cheek, "fixed" the Meeting. Rufus Jones and Douglas Steere agreed not to speak; the head football coach, who had *never* spoken in Meeting, agreed to say a few words. And so it happened, and much money later changed hands. Gilbert White, a deeply honest man, subsequently admitted what he had done and explained why (*not* in Meeting for Worship).

A Few Actual Meetings for Worship

As I have explained, students at Haverford College greatly resented it in the days when Fifth Day Meeting was required, even though, before entering the college, each had signed a statement accepting compulsory attendance. Students used to read books and magazines quite conspicuously, and turn the pages noisily. A visiting lecturer at Harverford reports on a Meeting at Haverford:

- "I was... delightfully surprised to find that Meeting was quiet and orderly.... There was a minimum of studying and reading. Douglas Steere, profession of philosophy, spoke on Sir William Osler [1849-1919; a brilliant teacher of medicine at McGill, the

University of Pennsylvania, John Hopkins, and Oxford] and his ministry to the whole man. Then Arnold Post, professor of Greek, added some comments about his acquaintance with Sir William.

"The Meeting seemed to end when a student arose and declaimed: 'This is my last compulsory Meeting for Worship at Haverford College, and I am glad of it. I want to make it clear that although I am a member of the Society of Friends, I consider this a travesty of worship and a terrible imposition on the students of this college. I hope that succeeding generations of Haverford students will rise up and practice that non-violent passive resistance on Friends which the latter have so successfully practiced on others.'

"A small interval elapsed and another student arose and said, 'I also am happy that this is my last Meeting for Worship, but for a different reason. As you know I am a fundamentalist, and I have missed hearing in this Meeting about the saving power of the blood of Jesus.'

"By this time the tension in the room was almost at the breaking point. It was difficult to see how the meeting would end. At this juncture, William Bacon Evans [noted peculiar Quaker wit mentioned earlier] arose from his position on the facing bench and intoned solemnly: 'No man descends so low in the scale of social values as to admit that he comes from New Jersey.'

"The ensuing laughter almost split the rafters, but Bacon Evans went on to say, 'And so it is with the Society of Friends, many of whose member seem to take special delight in concealing the fact that their beliefs have anything to do with the main body of Christendom.' "**

- A reported Meeting at Germantown Friends School, April 1988:

    Senior (who had attended GFS since kindergarten, a hard worker, wrestler, and one who had never spoken in Meeting before): "The most important virtue people can have is honor, keeping one's word. This is shown vividly in an old Clint Eastwood film. Doing good is not enough. Maintaining honor is more important. Eastwood broke the law, but he was a man of honor, hard-nosed tough. So was Humphrey Bogart [1899-1957] in *The African Queen* [1954]. Let's not worry about doing good. Be honest."

- *The school Head:* "I have been thinking about what Jesse said. I'm sure we all have. He is right. Keeping your word and honor are very important. They are forms of goodness that are different from being a do-gooder. Despite the context of violence, Jesse reminds us of some truths. You can read them in the Hebrew and Christian Bibles. I hope all of you will make time to become engaged with the prophets and kings and queens of the Old Testament, and the prophets and apostles in the New Testament. They, too, are people who act strongly. When they sin, they sin greatly. They defiantly turn away from God, which is what sin is, but then they alternately embrace God in such a heated way that it makes mere mortals such as us seem lukewarm.

**Adapted from *The Wit and Wisdom of William Bacon Evans* by Anna Cox Brinton. Pendle Hill Pamphlet, 1966, Wallingford, PA 19086

"It is no accident that the Westerns of our contemporary culture are so evocative of the traditions which are our heritage. Yes, Jesse, yes, all of you, keep your word, keep your honor."

- An older Friend reports a Meeting for Worship at Germantown Friends School during the time when Alex Haley's *Roots* was being serialized on TV: "It was a popcorn Meeting when mostly Black kids spoke one after another giving examples of **'you whites did this to me....'** Then an older Friend arose and, either because she had not heard or wanting to change the spirit of the Meeting, spoke about something scriptural which was entirely different from the theme. As soon as she sat down, an eighth grader popped up and said, 'Well, getting back to the subject....' and continued. Several speakers later, a Jewish student said simply, **'I'm shook; I'm really shook,'** and then a student said **'My father is Black and my mother is White. It makes me feel great conflicts inside. But I know, you all must know, that Black and White must be reconciled.'**

  "Then, as Meeting was about to close, a greatly respected math teacher, who is Black and married to a White man, and whose children, as one of them wrote a few years later, are 'a little bit white,' said 'Please look! We have to look ahead. Anger and hostility will get us nowhere. We have to learn to forgive.'"

- Upper School Meeting at Germantown Friends School:

  Black student: "People ask me why I am always so happy. I didn't used to be. I went to a Catholic school. A nun told me: 'Imagine this is the last day of life on Earth.' We students never discussed it. We all kidded and laughed. We decided to be happy. Here at GFS we're too tense, teachers included. So [big smile], be happy!"

  History and Quakerism teacher: "St. Augustine [354-430], the great saint, bishop, writer of <u>Confessions</u>, a classic of mysticism, and <u>The City of God</u>, when asked once what he was going to do next, replied, 'Weed my garden.'"

  Student on facing bench: "As I sat here, and as I stand now, I have a view of all of you. Quite a few of you are playing with your jewelry. I wear lots of jewelry. The jewels of gifts from my grandparents, my aunt, my parents. One I bought myself. I love all my jewels. Do I wear my heart on my sleeve? Well, yes, in my jewels."

  Student: "I am happy! I am glad I go here to school. We have courses; we have music, we have Meeting. We all are romantic. We all are idealists. I'm happy!"

  Teacher of Spanish: "One day I was at home with my former boyfriend. Suddenly, the door burst open, and a big, burly man with old trousers and an enormous beard burst in. I was terribly afraid. The man went up to me, gave me a big hug, and said, 'You must be Marjie!'

  "He was a friend of a friend, and he went about doing good, making people happy—both in Seattle and here. He made his living building boats in the Caribbean. One day he was swimming and met a shark. He was filled with adrenalin and managed to leap into his boat.

  "Well, later he died of leukemia and a memorial service was held for him in this Meetinghouse. It was sad. Everyone wept. But it was a celebration of a life. Life is good and beautiful."

- At Moorestown Friends Meeting, New Jersey, about halfway between New York and Washington, there was arranged a special Meeting for Worship for some children from East Germany. It was part of a movement called Kids for Peace. The students from Moorestown Friends School and the East German students, along with teachers, of course, entered the Meetinghouse. A teacher explained to everyone what a "silent Meeting" is, and then the Meeting for Worship began. Three German students spoke—really from the heart—and it became clear that the Mayor of New York had been rather rude to them. They said how much this Meeting meant to them. They would always remember it.

Someone present remembered a Moorestown student whispering to his bench-neighbor, "Gee, they don't *look* like Communists!"

Who's a Communist? Who's a Capitalist? We'll not discuss that now, but rather, move on to Business.

Chapter VIII:
Quaker Meetings for Business—Sometimes Risky

When the Quaker movement had its beginnings in England in the mid- seventeenth century, it was really an *un*organization, groups of seekers opposed to the religious and social formulas of the day. Early Friends fully expected, as a movement, to change the nature of Christianity, not merely to start a new Christian sect. They were "publishers of Truth" who believed, as I explained earlier, not in "a hireling ministry" but instead, in the words of founder George Fox [1624-1691], that "Christ has come to teach His people himself," and *today*, and that men and women did not need an organizational apparatus, budgets, elaborate buildings, or preachers in order to experience and act upon "the true Light that lighteth every man that cometh into the world."

Getting Organized

However Quakers—as the world called them—did get organized, and Fox took the lead in setting up a system of Monthly, Quarterly, and Yearly Meetings for doing business. And today these Meetings for Business are better called "Meetings for Worship for Business," since, in theory at least, Meetings for Business are conducted in a spirit of worship. They start and end with a period of worship, and when things get difficult, the clerk—the one who presides over the Meetings for Business—will sometimes call for a brief period of worship to seek truth and unity on the question under discussion.

Faith and Practice

In most Yearly Meetings, there is a book, carefully put together and, over the years, much revised, titled *Faith and Practice*. The Philadelphia Yearly Meeting version is 228 pages long, with sections covering everything from "Value and Use of the Bible," "The Peace Testimony," "Education," "Discouragement," to "Revision of *Faith and Practice*." And, speaking of such revision, in the sessions of Yearly Meeting preparing the 1972 revision, a hot question was where to place the section on "Sexuality"—because Friends, as far as I know, are as sexual as members any of any other religious body. Finally Mary Hoxie Jones made a suggestion that satisfied everyone: it should be placed between the section on "Marriage" and that on "Home and Family."

So in *Faith and Practice* the rules and regulations are carefully set down—even including "Stewardship of our Means," but most Friends do not accept *Faith and Practice* as absolute, wanting to avoid "the killing letter" of the law. The brief preface to the book quotes an epistle from the Meeting of Elders in Yorkshire, dated 1656:

> DEARLY BELOVED FRIENDS, these things we do not lay upon you as a rule of form to walk by, but that by all measure of light which is pure and holy [you] may be guided, and so in the light walking and abiding these may be fulfilled in the Spirit—not from the letter, for the letter killeth, but the Spirit giveth life.

Sense of the Meeting

Meetings for Business do not make their decisions on the basis of a vote of the members present. Rather they try to reach "a sense of the Meeting," a decision with which all can agree. During the discussions, members do not attempt to win an argument, but rather to reach the best decision with which all can unite. Some non-Friends call it trying to reach consensus, but it is more than consensus. However, I remember, while on a hike together in the White Mountains, New Hampshire, I asked a good friend who works with religious organizations in Rome what he thought Hell was. He answered without a moment's hesitation, "Watching a group of Quakers seeking consensus." (He went on to say that he agreed with all Friends' social principles but didn't like attending Meeting for Worship—that he was more a Friend than anything else.)

Sometimes, if a sense of the Meeting cannot be reached, the solution is to form a committee, and Friends are prone to form committees. In fact, I think it was a Friend who, frustrated by the lengthiness of the committee process, said, "The ideal committee is a committee of two with one absent," and another Friend, unhappy at the sometimes lengthy and unrealistic statements of committee on practical subjects, said that "a camel is an animal made by a committee." But the latter Friend was wrong in his estimation of the practicality of camels, given their environment, and wrong, too, about the consensus-seeking statements of Friends' committees. They usually work and keep the members united.

However at the end of one tangled and difficult Meeting for Business discussion, where a decision simply had to be reached, a Friend summed up the situation thus: "We just have to go forward, and we can hope that the way will open ahead of us at least as fast as it closes in behind us."

Some Incidents in Meetings for Business— a Mix of Wonderful Humorous, Outrageous

The "Social Room" of Germantown Meeting is where Meetings for Business are held. Once, during a rather dull discussion, I noticed a sign posted over the small collection of Quaker books available for borrowing. It read: PLEASE RETURN BOOKS WITHIN 3 WEEKS ... OR WE WILL SEND A GENTLE REMINDER. Yes, Friends are often gentle, but not always, for many have vigorous minds and spirits. Also their buildings are not always in perfect repair. Consider the following:

- A Meeting was raising funds for a new Meetinghouse, and the clerk was calling on members for pledges. One weighty, affluent, but tightfisted Friend rose and said, "I'll subscribe five dollars." Just then a piece of old plaster fell on his head. Half stunned, the weighty Friend mumbled, "I mean f-five hundred dollars."

- At another Meeting for Business, a humorous, weighty, wise Friend told the group that when it comes to fund-raising, what we all need is more practice and less faith.

Here are some other less physical incidents:

- On an Easter Sunday at the Brooklyn Friends Meeting someone called for a hymn (which was done from time to time there) and we sang "Were You There When They Crucified My Lord?" A long silence followed and then Harold Chance, a well-known peace worker for the American Friends Service Committee, rose and asked, "Were we there when they crucified our Lord—or were we at a Quaker committee meeting?"
  Of course, Harold recognized the importance of committee work in the Society of Friends but was challenging us on our priorities. The message was unforgettable.

- Harold J. Morland, clerk of London Yearly Meeting in 1929, sometimes allowed his wit to play on Friends who were voluble in business meetings. Henry T. Hodgkin was present that year on a furlough from his missionary duties in China, and Friends listened gladly when he spoke. The clerk alone was conscious of the passage of time, and, rising as Henry took his seat, he said, "It is a great pleasure to have Henry Hodgkin at home again and taking part in his Yearly Meeting. It is, I think, nine years since he was here last. There can be no impropriety in his speaking to us for a period of twenty minutes. If we divide twenty by nine or ten, does it not suggest a proper limit of time for regular attenders?"

- Alfred Scattergood, a banker and clear-thinking substantial Friend, was clerk of Germantown Meeting. At one session when the discussion seemed to be getting nowhere, Alfred raised his hand for silence, looked impressively around the room and said, "I think Friends are pawing the air." As I remember, the Meeting got back on track and quickly reached several sound decisions.

- Alfred Scattergood could be wryly humorous. Not only was he clerk and a banker, but he also had a raft of children. One Wednesday evening, Meeting for Business was scheduled as usual for 7:45. It was cold and snowy. At 7:50 Alfred, a stickler for punctuality, had not yet arrived, and the group settled into the customary period of silent worship. After about five minutes, the door opened, Alfred entered, and worship ended. As he made his way to the clerk's seat behind the table facing the members, someone said, "Well, Alfred, did thee get them all to bed?"

"Yes I did," replied Alfred, "and their galoshes with them."

- In 1952, the second Friends World Conference was held at Oxford, England, with several hundred people in attendance from the United States, the British Isles, and several other parts of the globe. They represented not only a variety of cultures, but also many different theological, economic, social, and political points of view. Hence the Epistle Committee recommended that no general statement be issued from that gathering.

   When that recommendation was presented at a plenary session of that Conference, there was considerable opposition to it and dissension developed. In the midst of that tension, Barrow Cadbury, an eminent Friend in his 90's, rose from his seat on the platform and prayed a most remarkable petition. His brief and moving words were: "We are in a terrible fix, Oh God. Help Thou us."

   A tremendous quiet developed following those words and soon a spirit of unity arose in favor of issuing a statement. Within a few moments the clerk was able to gather "the sense of the meeting" and declare that a General Epistle would be issued.

   Such is the way in which some stormy business sessions eventually arrived at general agreement, arising from a spirit of worship.

- At Meeting for Business, the question of whether business meetings should not be held on Wednesdays at 7:45-10:00,* when younger members who had small children were finding it difficult to attend because of family responsibilities. Would it not be better to hold Monthly Meeting right after Sunday Meeting for Worship, with a few minutes out for the quick eating of a sandwich between worship and business? A wise and weighty Friend and noted surgeon, as well as a clear-minded concise consensus promoter, stated that he thought it would be wise to continue to hold Meeting for Business after dinner, because good food raises the blood sugar, and people are more likely to reach consensus when their blood sugar is high.

- Monthly Meeting was discussing what had become a real problem on Sundays during Meeting for Worship. It was that during the hour-long Meeting, some person was sneaking into the Social Room and stealing coats and other valuables. Obviously some signs were needed to warn Friends of this fact and suggest that they take their coats and valuables into Meting with them. So the question: Who should make the signs? The obvious answer was the Property Committee. However, someone expressed a brilliant idea: "How about the Outreach Committee?"

- When people apply to become members of the Society of Friends—that is, to join a Monthly Meeting—they must do so in writing. Their letter is read to Monthly

---

* Ten o'clock is generally called "Quaker midnight."

Meeting and then two or three members are appointed to visit the prospective Friend. They then report to Monthly Meeting, usually recommending acceptance of the person into membership. However Friends do not act hastily, and the application is allowed to "lie on the table" for a month so that Friends can become acquainted with the applicant. At one such Monthly Meeting session in Germantown, people asked where the applicant usually sat so they could identify her and get to know her. The clerk answered, "Well, she's about thirty years old, has a couple of kids, and sits about three benches back in the graveyard quadrant of the Meetinghouse." (A graveyard is across the Meetinghouse driveway on the left, rear side of the building.)

- The annual business meeting of the American Friends Service committee was just gathering into a period of worship on November 22, 1963, when the chairman, Harold Evans, rose and announced the report of the shooting of President John F. Kennedy in Dallas, Texas. It was not yet know whether the President was mortally wounded. Harold Evans also announced that a staff member was remaining in the office to listen on the radio for further news.

  One of those attending reported, "The stunned audience gathered into one of the most moving Meetings for Worship I have ever experienced. All of us were concentrated in the unspoken prayer that our President might live. After what seemed an eternity, Louis Schneider, executive secretary of the AFSC, walked into the room, up to Harold Evans. Lou's face was grim, and as he approached Harold Evans he shook his head. And so we knew that John Kennedy was dead.

  "The Meeting then became more poignant, if that was possible. The several hundred people were not individuals but one person asking for an answer for the unanswerable, trying to cope with the anguish, the shock."

- A special all-day series of sessions of a Meeting were organized on the theme, "The Meaning of Simplicity." Such sessions could be called, in a sense, business meetings since, although periods of worship are a part of them, a statement is usually drafted, agreed to, and issued at the end. Well, Friends had been talking about the dangers of cluttered lives, the importance of total disarmament, and various direct and simple solutions to problems of war, race, hunger, etc. For one Friend, all of this was too much: simple thinking about complex subjects. So during a period of worship toward the end of the day he stood and said, **"Talking about and advocating simple solutions to vastly complex situations is dangerous. We should remember the words of Oscar Wilde, 'The truth is seldom plain and never simple.' So, Friends, beware of simplicity!"**

- During World War II, many Quakers were conscientious objectors and refused to participate in the war. The government recognized their rights of conscience and set up Civilian Public Service (CPS) camps to which CO's were sent to do "work of national importance under civilian direction." Although the CPS camps were not directed by the military, they were visited by military officers from time to time.

  In 1944, at a CPS camp in Mancos, Colorado, there was a practice among Quaker CO's to hold a sort of business session after breakfast when a CO would present a "thought for the day."

On the day I write about, Corbet Bishop, a CO bookseller from Alabama, arose and said he had some important ideas he wanted to share. It happened to be a day when there were a number of military officers visiting. Corbet then read his statement which was strongly patriotic and emphasized—in a flag-waving manner—that everyone owes this great nation his service and devotion. He referred to "our great and noble armed forces" and ended with another appeal to patriotism.

The ending was so movingly patriotic that the military men broke out into strong applause. When the applause had died down, Corbet Bishop stated: "I have just read a passage from *Mein Kampf* by Adolf Hitler."

-oOo-

This CPS "meeting for business" was, obviously, far from typical, even though it ended in a strange period of silence and even though a point was made, perhaps not in an entirely loving manner. So, to come back to more serious matters, or at least more prudent ones, I think it is interesting to point out that in business and government committees, more and more groups are using the technique of seeking consensus, not for religious reasons, but because decisions reached in this manner are more workable, mature, constructive, and energy-producing than are sessions where the main effort is to win the argument. People come out of the sessions in agreement, having thought things through thoroughly, and therefore ready to work with enthusiasm to achieve important goals.

Chapter IX: Quaker Weddings and Memorial Services

A Quaker wedding or a Quaker memorial service is a specially called Meeting for Worship. In both of them there is a considerable element of the unprogrammed, and therefore and element of risk—less so, however, than in a regular Sunday Meeting for Worship. There is no doubt that at a wedding the couple will marry each other. And there is no double that at a memorial service those who gather for worship will center upon the life of the deceased person and the meaning of life and death. The emphasis is, respectively, on the *couple* being married or the *person* who had died, not on a fixed order of service.

Quaker Weddings

As I suggested above, part of a Friends' wedding is established. Before the marriage, the couple must have the approval of the Monthly Meeting, must "pass Meeting." They are visited by a Committee on Clearness, who discuss with them the meaning and responsibilities of marriage and make sure that they are not already married. Overseers of the wedding are appointed—often Friends who are known by the couple—and are in charge of the proceedings, but, of course, not of the period of unprogrammed worship which follows the exchange of promises between the couple: "In the presence of God and these our friends, I take thee _____ to be my wife/husband, promising with divine assistance to be unto thee a loving and faithful wife/husband so long as we both shall live."*

---

*Here, for those interested, is the text of the marriage certificate prescribed by Philadelphia Yearly Meeting's *Faith and Practice*, and sometimes gently modified by the prospective bride and groom:

Whereas, A.B., of _____, son of C.B. and H.B., of _____, and D.E., of _____, daughter of F.E. and M.E., of _____, having declared their intentions of marriage with each other to

_____ Monthly Meeting of the Religious Society of Friends held at _____, their proposed marriage was allowed by that Meeting.

Now this is to certify to whom it may concern, that for the accomplishment of their intentions, this _____ day of the _____ month, in the year of our Lord, _____, they, A.B. and D.E., appeared in a meeting for worship of the Religious Society of Friends, held at _____, and A.B. taking D.E. by the hand, did, on this solemn occasion, declare that he took her, D.E., to be his wife, promising with Divine assistance to be unto her a loving and faithful husband so long as they both shall live; and then, in the same assembly D.E. did in like manner declare that she took him, A.B., to be her husband, promising with Divine assistance to be unto him a loving and faithful wife so long as they both shall live. And moreover they, A.B. and D.E., she, according to the custom of marriage, assuming the surname of her husband, did, as further confirmation thereof, then and there, to this certificate set their hands.

        A.B._____
        D.E.B._____

And we, having been present at the marriage, have as witnesses hereunto set our hands.

After a couple have exchanged promises, an overseer or someone specially chosen, reads a certificate stating what just happened, and the bride and groom sign it. *Then* comes the period of unprogrammed worship, typically lasting from thirty to forty-five minutes, and then closed by two of the overseers shaking hands.

Variations

Sometimes the couple may wish to have music played or sung by a person or small group while people are gathering in the Meetinghouse before the ceremony begins. Also the couple may ask that certain passages from the Bible or other meaningful literature be read either before or after the exchange of promises. In addition, especially if many of the attenders at the wedding are unfamiliar with Friends' procedures, one of the overseers will explain to all what is going to happen and especially about the unprogrammed period of worship during which anyone present may be "led" to speak.

There are some splendid sorts of variations. I shall describe only one such, which was the wedding of my wife's and my daughter, Becky, to a Jew, Larry. Both were enthusiastic about having a Quaker wedding, but they wanted some special things so that the spirit and delights of Jewish weddings might also be included. All of these were approved by the overseers appointed by the Meeting. Therefore:

- After all had gathered in the Meetinghouse, Larry's father read a wonderful paper he had written for the occasion, explaining the deep significance of the institution of the family in Jewish religion and culture.

- When Becky and Larry exchanged their promises, they did not simply stand and do so but walked a few steps into the broad aisle of the Meetinghouse and stood under a chuppa, the traditional cloth canopy held over the couple by four family members—in this case both Larry's and Becky's family.

- Then came the period of unprogrammed worship with much delightful speaking. When the appropriate time had come to end the period of worship and speaking, a quiet signal was given and seven members of the now-joint family recited the seven traditional Jewish blessings, which are universal in their truth and as meaningful for Quakers as for Jews. They are:

    You abound in blessings, Lord our God, Source of all creation, Creator of the fruit of the vine.

    You abound in blessings, Lord our God, Source of all creation, all of whose creations reflect your glory.

    You abound in blessings, Lord our God, Source of all creation, Creator of human beings.

    You abound in blessings, Lord our God, Source of all creation, who created man and woman in Your image that they might live, love, and so perpetuate life.

    We all rejoice as these two people, overcoming separateness, unite in joy. May rejoicing resound throughout the world as the homeless are given homes, persecution and oppression cease, and all people learn to live in peace with each other and in harmony with the earth.

    May these lovers rejoice as did the first man and woman in the Garden of Eden. You abound in blessings, Lord, Source of joy for bride and groom.

    We acknowledge the Unity of all, and we celebrate today joy and gladness, bridegroom and bride, delight and cheer, love and harmony, peace and companionship. May we all witness the day when the sounds throughout the world will be the sounds of happiness, the voices of lovers, the sounds of feasting and singing. Praised is love; blessed be this marriage. May the bride and bridegroom rejoice together.

- Then, after the withdrawal of the wedding party, came the shaking of hands.

Risks

I said earlier that there are some risks involved in Quaker weddings. Here are eight examples:

- The mother of the bride, not a Friend, was terribly concerned that there should be no unseemly display of emotion, especially weeping with joy, during the wedding. She even wanted to pay to have a weighty and famous Friend come to the wedding and speak. (The Friend tactfully refused.) Well, it was a wonderful wedding, but, yes, during the unprogrammed part, a close friend of the bride and groom was so moved as she spoke about love and the couple who were now married that her voice choked with emotion, and other sounds of deep joy were heard in the Meetinghouse.

- During a wedding, a sweet-looking elderly lady, a member of the Meeting, stood and wished the young couple good luck. Then she proceeded for what seemed like fifteen minutes to enumerate all the perils and problems of marriage. When she sat down, Friends and non-Friends felt that the couple would indeed need good luck.

- A Friend stood and said, "The secrets for the success of my wife's and my happy marriage are two: complementary stupidities (I'd hate to be married to myself) and free snarling (what could be duller than 'We've been married for twenty years and never had a cross word!') Of course, it helps, too, to have the stupidities and the snarling undergirded by love."

- A young girl, perhaps ten, stood and said strongly, "Well, all I can say is that I hope X and X will be more happily married than my parents seem to be, even though they stick together."

- A now-married Quaker woman wrote this: "One of the things that I always liked about being a Quaker was that my husband and I would marry each other. The idea that it would be a 'group effort' involving everyone who attended, fascinated me.

    "During our wedding, I looked around the Meetinghouse, and one person that I couldn't place was an *elderly woman sitting with my family*. Since most of my 'extended' family either lived too far away or were boycotting my wedding, I couldn't figure out who she could be. Towards the end of the Meeting she got up and started talking. All I could make sense of her message was the part where she compared my wife and me to *Romeo and Juliet*. Considering how that play ended I wasn't sure that it was an appropriate comparison.

    "After we broke Meeting (punctuated with a yell of '*Mazel Tov*', [Yiddish for 'Congratulations!' or 'Good luck!'] from the *Romeo and Juliet* lady), we had a small reception. After some investigative work, I finally found out who she was: a *shopping bag lady*. She had come to the Christmas breakfast at the Meetinghouse the week before and had found out about our wedding. I was more than amused. I mean, not everyone has a shopping bag lady at their wedding. My mother thought it was wonderful. To her, it was a sign of good fortune. I'm not sure about that. What I am pretty sure of, however, is that she *liberated a couple of wedding presents*. I hope we have the same china pattern."

Quakers in general, as far as I can tell, seem more likely to stay married than is the general population. One reason for this may be lack of haste in making the decision and the thinking needed to "pass Meeting." An example is a story sent to me by a British Friend about a young Friend in Maryland many years ago: "He was rather shy about proposing to Anna, the daughter of a Quaker family next door. He went on being in love with her for almost eleven years. He built a house and all the outhouses to go with it. One day he invited Anna's family over to see the property and showed to them everything. The relatives saw to it that Anna was left alone with him and nothing happened. Finally, he took her to the outbuilding and leaning over the pigsty, which was empty, looked at her affectionately and said, 'Anna, shall we buy a pig?' He bought the pig, they were then married, and they lived happily ever after. People do propose in the quaintest of places."

- I'm not sure that this item ever was told during a Quaker wedding, but it might well have been. An attractive, humorous, able, elderly spinster was asked by a member of her Meeting in an informal moment, just after meeting, "Agnes, how is it that thee never married?"

  Agnes smiled at the questioner and replied, "Well, thee knows, it takes a mighty good husband to be better than none."

- One might also say, "It takes a mighty good wedding to be better than none." Despite the fact that if all procedures are properly followed, a Quaker wedding is totally legal, recognized, and binding. There are some—especially when one of the partners is not a Friend—who have their doubts. At a wedding in Orange Grove, New Jersey, the couple, just to be sure, were married also the day before by a minister at a small church in a park.

  At another Quaker wedding, I think in New Jersey, the clerk of the Meeting was asked in a loud voice, "Is this legal?"

  And yet another couple had a wonderful Quaker wedding service, but then they rushed downtown to be married also by a justice of the peace, and then rushed to the reception.

-oOo-

Quaker Memorial Services

The Clerk of our Germantown Monthly Meeting and I are very good friends, and for years we were also colleagues as teachers. Occasionally, if either of us gets to feeling discouraged, I will say to Pat or Pat to me, "Well, if you get really discouraged, I'll tell you what I think I'll say at your memorial service," and just that cheers us up. Neither of us, yet, has got so discouraged that we've felt the need to ask, "Well, O.K., I need to hear what you will say."

On the other side, less cheerful, there was a memorial service for a very unpleasant, prickly Friend in a rather small rural Meeting. After Friends had gathered, there was an embarrassingly long period of total silence, which was finally broken by someone standing and saying, "Well, you'll have to admit it. Sometimes Alfred wasn't half as mean as he usually was."

-oOo-

- A Friend, Margaret, who had suffered for years from Parkinson's disease, becoming a ghost of her original vigorous, humorous, productive self. At last she died, and those who spoke at her memorial service remembered in great and small ways the Margaret they had known during her prime years of life. At the very end her daughter rose and said, **"I feel as if my mother has been given back to me, not taken away. She has been brought back to life."**

- It was in Fritchley Meeting [England] that I heard the most moving words which I remember hearing spoken in Meeting. My parents' nearest neighbors were a couple of Fritchley Friends who kept a vegetarian guest house, Arthur and Katie Ludlow. She was the moving spirit of the two, much loved and respected. She had a trim little figure, a manner quiet, but capable of animation, and a general bearing which bespoke the Quakeress. They had two children: Elsie and Wilfred. At the age of nineteen, Wilfred was killed on his motorbike, and very soon after Elsie went into a decline and died before long. We were all shattered by this tragedy. The Sunday after Elsie's death, Katie Ludlow was at Meeting, as trim as ever in her Quaker-grey, sitting in her normal place, facing the meeting. After an initial silence she rose to her feet and said simply: **"The Lord has given, and the Lord has taken away."** [Job 1:21] She then sat down.

- An American Friend, Ruth Dross, died at the age of eighty-two. She was born in Stuttgart, Germany, and worked for many years with Quaker and also Episcopal organizations. She had a *very* clear mind and, when called upon to do so, spoke her mind clearly, directly, and usefully—whether in German or in English.

    At her memorial service, when the Chestnut Hill Meetinghouse in Philadelphia was crowded with those whose lives she had influenced, many stories were told about her life and work, and her wise humor.

    One Friend recalled Ruth saying to a group, **"You Americans, and especially Quakers, have a disease. It is <u>committees</u>! Whenever you don't know what to do, you form a committee. Well, Jesus said, 'Behold, I am in your mist.' I say to you Quakers, in our often confused committees, 'I am in your midst; and I hope things will clear up!'** Ruth said this knowing very well that in German the word <u>Mist</u> means <u>manure</u>."

    A delighted laugh of recognition of truth was heard throughout the Meetinghouse.

- At the triennial celebration of the establishment of the Friends World Committee on Consultation, held in Kenya, about a hundred people met for worship together in an unprogrammed Meeting for Worship. During the Meeting, an older woman, black and wearing a white turban, entered and, after finding a place, just wept and wept. Everyone there was aware of it, and the Meeting focused on sorrow, comfort, and compassion. Everyone there—from many nations— reached out to the woman.

    Later, Friends learned that the weeping woman was the mother of a son who was a Quaker, and a lawyer, in Nairobi, and had defended a person in trouble with the government. Suddenly agents of the government had swooped down in the middle of the night, taken him away, and he had "dropped off the world." The woman had been up all night, but finally had the courage to ask for help, and her son—after eighteen months in solitary confinement with no bed, only a Bible—was released. Later Haverford College awarded him an honorary LLD degree.

- It is interesting that in Friends schools, if a classmate dies, quite often his or her classmates—even though the vast majority of them are not Quakers—want nothing more than to hold a Quaker memorial service (in latter days, they may call it "getting together for a Meeting for Worship to remember Katie"). And they do gather "in the Meetinghouse," they share, and they are comforted.

  But this is true also of very young students. If a beloved teacher dies, the children say, "We need to go to the Meetinghouse," and they do and share memories and appreciation. I know of a fourth grade class that recently did this, and a first grade class.

- The son of a faithful, brilliant Quaker couple, suddenly died at age ten. Tom was a beautiful, intellectual, friendly boy. I remember visiting his fourth-grade classroom at Germantown Friends School and seeing him, amid the lively proceedings of the class, lying on a patch of carpet on the floor, reading a book, undistracted by the wholesome noises of learning going on around him.

  After Tom's death, a marvelous and moving memorial service was held, and, at the end, his mother stood, her husband tightly holding her hand, and said, **"Please keep remembering Tom, keep his spirit alive in your hearts."**

  The whole Meeting wept together. It was truly a communion service.

- At a memorial service in Moorestown, New Jersey, for a strong-charactered Friend who died when she was well over ninety, there was message after message about all the kind of things that Lydia had done for the speakers. And all of her children spoke, including one who said, in love, **"And she was hard to get along with"**—which meant, all understood: She was a woman of strong character.

- One of the most moving memorial services, for me, was that of my mother, Edith Warner Johnson. She died at age eighty-four. She had always been a poet, and up until the last week of her life in the medical center of a retirement community, she was busy working on her poems—revising, revising, revising. After her death, a memorial service was held at Haverford Meeting, near Philadelphia. Many people spoke in deep appreciation of her humorous, deep, loving nature. And then I felt "called" to read one of her poems, "Offshore."*

---

* See footnote on page 30.

OFFSHORE

The wind is blowing off the shore
Out to sea.
"No more, no more," it sighs to me.

I have no sail to set me free;
My craft is small, manned by me.
My mast is broken, gone the oar.

The wind is blowing off the shore
Out to sea.
"No more, no more," it sighs to me.

No more wave-lap on the shore—
Is that a light out there I see?

My reading of this poem was followed by a deep and loving silence, and then the Meeting for Worship was closed by those in charge shaking hands.

-oOo-

Quaker weddings and memorial services are, as you can see, "gathered" by the marriage of two people or the death of a beloved member. Now we come to Meetings for Worship that seem to be gathered by a force—spiritual? intellectual? holy? God-given? need-based? inspirational?—broader than those reported in this chapter.

Chapter X: Some "Gathered" Meetings for Worship

It is nearly impossible to explain, let alone define, the term "gathered Meeting." It can mean a Meeting where, suddenly or gradually, all the members feel brought together by the Spirit (or *spirit,* if you're not very God-minded). Rufus Jones was quoted in a Meeting at Hockessin, Delaware, as saying, "A Meeting ought to be like the rising of water in a lock, which enables the ship to go out for its journey on a higher level." Many Meetings for Worship are like that—and many aren't. Or it can mean a Meeting in which someone expresses an idea, raises a question, or tells of an experience which sets the tone and theme for the Meeting and following speakers add their thoughts and inspirations. Sometimes such Meetings are rather intellectual, sometimes emotional, but more often a combination of both.

Brief Examples and Explanations

A Friend recalls a Meeting that was a "Baptism experience." She writes:

- Our Alice was born January 16, so around Christmas, I was truly "great with child". The Sunday before Christmas, the whole Meeting for Worship centered around the miracle of birth, of a new life.

Leonard Kenworthy regrets that the citation of poetry or passages from the Bible have become quite rare in recent years, and their gathering effects, therefore, reduced. He writes, however, about Ruth Vail, a resident of a Quaker-run retirement community, Kendal at Longwood, Pennsylvania, who recently died at age 101. She was blind but mentally very alert. Says Leonard:

- Toward the close of Meeting for Worship, Ruth Vail frequently rises and recites a brief passage of poetry from her vast store of such choice words, and then adds a few words of intense supplication in the form of prayer. In that way she helps to "cover" the Meeting and to "gather" it in a powerful way.

Another aspect of the gatheredness of a Meeting also took place at Kendal. A Friend reports:

- I attended a Meeting for Worship with a member of my family and began thinking of the well-known message of George Fox. "There is that of God in every one." Before I felt ready to give a message, my guest stood up and began his message with the words, "There is that of God in every one."

    I was impressed again with the value of our Quaker Meetings for Worship, where in the silence "that of God" speaks to us, or through us, to our neighbors. It is not uncommon for a common inspiration or concern to arise from the Meeting and be shared.

Yet another gathered Meeting took place during the Viet Nam War (1954-75), about 1970. It was at the headquarters of the American Friends Service Committee in Philadelphia, and the Board of Directors of this major Quaker service organization was having a deep, heartfelt, and divided discussion about whether the AFSC should send medical aid to Hanoi, which would be civil disobedience and a crime: giving aid to the enemy. The Clerk of the board then asked that Friends enter into a period of worship, and from the silence gradually developed a gatheredness, and the decision was made: send the aid, save lives.

In Germantown Meeting, over many decades, Grace Warner Waring always sat in a special place on the lowest facing bench of the Meetinghouse. She explained, "I like to see people's faces and hold people in the light." Even as she grew old, weak, and shaky, when she spoke in Meeting her voice, somehow empowered by God, was firm and full of vigor, reaching the very back benches. One memorable time, after a truly gathered silence, she rose and spoke two words: **"Listen! Listen!"**

Another Friend, now about forty-five-years-old, remembers:

- The first awareness of the silence of a gathered Meeting is almost overwhelming. The impact hit me emotionally as it did my father when I took him to Meeting. There can be all kinds of little noises—superficial ones, throat-clearing, shoes hitting bench. They become a part of the sound of silence and don't touch it. And the speaking arises so completely from the silence that the worship seems unbroken.

In 1988, on the campus of the International Christian University in Tokyo, there took place the celebration of the founding fifty-five years earlier of the Friends World Committee for Consultation. Simeon Shitemi, the Clerk of the celebration, reported "to Friends everywhere" the deep, multidimensional gatheredness of the Friends from thirty-five nations, who were "encouraged to be Earth citizens, not just citizens of the nations from which we came." He wrote:

- The multi-colored threads of our various forms of worship wove a rich pattern through the fabric of our sessions, giving us the confidence to face and express our own pains and conflicts. We ministered to each other singly, in small groups, and in plenary worship, giving and receiving inspiration, healing, and wisdom. Certain phrases resounded in our hearts. If our prayers are to be effective, we heard, we cannot lie to God or to ourselves; too often in pray we ask God to do for us what God is asking us to do, and we try to do ourselves what we should leave to God. Worship is the natural response of human beings to the sublime love of God reflected through Jesus Christ, we were told; worship and obedience as the whole of life. In such a context, Quaker service is a form of intercessory prayer. A Cuban Friend urged that we see our Meetinghouses not as garages but as service stations.

We are parting on our separate ways, planning reports, writing speeches, gathering photographs to share as widely as possible the showers of blessings that have been ours here in Tokyo. And we are parting gratefully certain that we are joined together by that One who is the silent center, the still point of our spinning world.

Herbert Bowles, a surgeon and member of Honolulu Friends Meeting, now "sojourning" in Germantown, remembers working in the area of Kinsan, South Korean, in 1958—mostly surgery but also helping with the construction of emergency housing and shelters for the chronically ill. He and British Friends were asked by some Koreans to have a Friends Meeting. He writes:

- A number of us, including Ham Suk Hon, a sedate elderly Friend, and several young Koreans who had been serving as interpreters decided to have a Friends Meeting. We were told first to go to a church service which was being held in a mission church. When we got there, there was no room for the large number of our interested people. However there was a large cemetery with a grassy slope overlooking it. A couple of very noisy boys, about ten years old, were playing near the slope where we decided to sit for our "Meeting." There was also a nanny goat and her two kids near where we were sitting. We didn't feel like scolding the noisy boys or chasing the goats away so we assembled, overlooking the cemetery. While we sat quietly, the boys gradually quieted down, and, without being summoned, came and sat down on the bank with us, not saying a word. The nanny goat and her two kids joined us and, except for an occasional bleat, were quiet, though moving about next to the seated attenders. One or two of the Koreans spoke during the Meeting, and it was agreed by all that we had had a very gratifying Friends Meeting although we had to meet outside of the church building.*

A Friend writes:

- When I was a freshman at Swarthmore College in 1937, it was the custom to have a fifteen-minute break in the middle of the morning. One could go to the bookstore, the post office or some other locale. The Swarthmore Friends Meetinghouse on the campus was also open at that time, and I often went there to sit alone in the Friendly silence and to collect my scattered thoughts. Occasionally another student, or perhaps a faculty member, would come. But most of the time I was there alone.

---

*Eventually Seoul Meeting of Friends was organized and exists today.

One day Dr. Frank Aydelotte, the president of the college, joined me—and spoke. I have no recollection of what he said, but it touched this green, country girl and made me feel important; I mattered!

Another Friend writes about a Meeting on a snowy day:

- An eighty-year-old Friend spoke about the great quiet in the city following the snow and the need to find the Center of quiet within ourselves. Then another spoke about visiting a small museum at the center of which was a small courtyard with daylight coming in from all four sides and in which bulbs in various stages of growth were planted. She spoke about the inner courtyard of ourselves. An interval passed and another recited the third verse of Whittier's hymn—the one that is often left out:
  "O Sabbath rest by Galilee,
  O calm of hills above
  Where Jesus knelt to share with Thee
  The silence of eternity
  Interpreted by Love."
  After a while, another spoke about the terrible things that are happening to people in the world and the necessity for coming out from the quiet center to act; that Jesus had times when he needed to be alone, and yet was able to act because of what had occurred during those periods when he was "at the center." Finally, another person quoted William James that it is almost impossible to remain concentrated on one thing over a period of time, but that discipline and strength are built from repeatedly bringing oneself back from distractions.

More Gathered Meetings

I now report, mostly on the basis of my attendance at them and notes I inconspicuously took, on the essential words spoken at a few gathered Meetings. Remember, reader, that these Meetings are usually about an hour long and that most often the first ten to twenty minutes are totally silent. The words I report arose from the silence.

Often, but not always, I knew the names of the speakers. I do not, however, use them in these reports. Instead, I indicate the sex and approximate age of each speaker.

- Man, 71 I was jogging last week, when a small group of little kids stopped me and asked, "How do we get to the big house near here, the one with old stone walls and a big blue door?"
  I replied, "I don't know, I'm afraid."
  Kid: "You're afraid?"
  Me: "No, I'm not afraid. I just don't know. Are you afraid?"
  Several kids: "Yeah; we sure are; often afraid."
  Me: "Well, what are you afraid of?"
  Kid: "Maybe I'll get lost and won't be able to get home."
  Kid: "Who's going to move in next door? Will it be bad people?"
  Kid: "Will my Dad ever come back. I'm afraid he won't and I need him."

Some "Gathered" Meetings for Worship

Kid: "I'm afraid of worms."

Well, I was startled by this long recital of fears. How can we deal with all this fear?

- *Woman, 43* I'm afraid much of the time. I wear two hearing aids—will I go deaf? I live alone. I don't own my house. If I get into deep trouble, who will take care of me?

- *Woman, 45* I was about to make a trip to Nicaragua to work with people there. Suddenly my doctor told me I needed a serious operation. I had to put off my trip and go to the hospital. I was afraid! Also, I needed to be fed by someone else—imagine, feed <u>me</u>, when I was going to help feed others. So I called my daughter who was about to go on a vacation. "I'm afraid," I said, "I can't manage." She replied, "O.K. I'll stay with you and not go on vacation." I felt guilty, and then I realized how important it is to <u>accept</u> help—almost as important as to give help.

- *Man, 75* Remember Jesus on the cross. At the ninth hour he cried in a loud voice, "My God, my God, why hast thou forsaken me?" Even Jesus ! Even he—afraid!

-oOo-

- *Man, 71* As I've been sitting in Meeting this morning, I've had a very unspiritual thought. It concerns itching. When a part of our body itches we have a totally self-centered and urgent need to <u>scratch</u>! Nothing is more urgent at that moment. How much of each of our lives is made up of the need to scratch itches?

- *Woman, 43* There is a German expression: <u>heilig Unruh</u>, the holy unrest—a sort of holy itch which knocks us off any comfortable place we may be occupying. Such an itch can be useful!

  However, recently I saw a TV program on death. It showed how the process of dying can be a falling away from life's itchiness (although they didn't use that word) into calm and peace and ecstasy.

- *Man, 48* Children are taught <u>not</u> to scratch, even an itch. It's not good manners. And we adults are even more taught. But itching is good, and the actions it causes are good.

  We are a young country, full of itches. Racism is a very deep American itch. We can scratch a bit and enjoy the luxury of a guilt trip. But our Congress has long had the itch of racism and is scratching its way toward justice. We blacks should recognize this. Remember, in our early days our laws allowed one race to seize the property of another race, and also to make some human beings mere property.

  I say: Let our good itches spread!

- *Man, 55* In the military, soldiers when in formation are not allowed to scratch. In the People's Music Network, the participants put their itches into song.

  My feeling is that we should not just do what we like to do, but learn to like what we <u>have</u> to do, so that we, with George Fox, can walk cheerfully over the earth answering that of God in every one.

- *Man, 22* The trouble with most of us is that we have itching palms. We are more interested in money and success than in finding the meaning of life. Me, I work for a public interest group, and we need <u>money</u> to do our work. That itch is a good one.

- *Woman, 35* I am a musician. Musicians itch. Itches are signals from our bodies, and all our bodies, together, responding, make a human symphony. Humanity is a symphony. But each of us must <u>care</u> for our instruments, ourselves, so that we can make the truest sounds in the symphony.

- *Woman, 41* Buddha expressed somewhat the same idea our Friend has just given us. He said that our right hand leads to and works for the immediate community; our left hand reaches for the horizon. We must "listen" to our hands and learn the proper balance between being receptive and expressive.

- *Man, 52* "By their <u>works</u> you shall know them." Our works, what we do—that's our note in life's itchy symphony. And by our works we can reach out to others. We need outreach.

- *Man, 75* When I was in elementary school many years ago, my principal told me, "Beverly, don't let the little things bother you." I have always found this advice very helpful.

- *Man, 73* A question we must all prayerfully consider is: Which community itch shall we scratch? For this we need the vertical dimension, that dimension of questioning prayer.

- *Woman, 21* A while ago, I was on a beach at three o'clock in the morning, and with the waves coming in, and the sand soft, and the dark immense, I asked myself, "What is religion?" I am a Catholic. To me ritual is important. But this morning in your Meeting I have found the answer: religion is what we do; it is more than the mystery of what we don't know. So be religious. Define your itch—and <u>do</u>!

-oOo-

Remember, reader, as you consider these accounts of gathered Meetings for Worship, that between each of the utterance is a period of silence, and silent reflection. A true Meeting for Worship is not a conversation.

-oOo-

- *Man, 86* Two hundred years ago today, George Washington was inaugurated President of the United States. He was a religious man, and the virtue he most greatly exemplified was integrity. And James Madison, the "master builder of the Constitution," was a strong advocate of the Bill of Rights, which guaranteed us religious freedom. Earlier than this, our own George Fox, in England, opened the way to universal religious practice, not according to any state-established formula. We all, now, all over the world, need to be more tolerant of universal religion, under the leadership and love of God.

Some "Gathered" Meetings for Worship

- *Man, 77* What our Friend has said brings to mind a wonderful old hymn:
  For the love of God is broader
  Than the measures of man's mind,
  And the heart of the Eternal
  Is most wonderfully kind.
  If <u>our</u> love were but more simple,
  We would take him at his word,
  And our lives would be all sunshine
  In the sweetness of our Lord.

- *Woman, 56* I have been moved by what we have heard in Meeting this morning, but I must unburden myself of concern about three events which seem so totally unloving. The first is the teenagers who raped and beat a jogger in New York, just out of hate. The second is the fact that I know two of our teachers bought lottery tickets; they gambled, which is contrary to Quaker principles, and what would they do with the money if they won? And the third is that we consider West Germany our enemy because they don't want American nuclear missiles stationed in their country.

- *Man, 78* One of my really great teachers was in First Day School here at this Meeting, William E. Cadbury. I remember he told us: "Liberty we should prize, but with liberty goes responsibility, and we must experience our liberty <u>within</u> the law."

  I am convinced that we all need a sense of values. Only with values can we rightly serve God and man.

- *Woman, 42* In these days of my life I want to <u>kneel</u>, I need to kneel—at my desk at home, <u>and</u> here in Meeting. As I kneel, I find that the pain in my life can be turned into joy—pain into joy and into a feeling of God. And so now I kneel [the Friend sank to her knees in an attitude of prayer] and express my thankfulness to this Meeting for its loving support.

- *Man, 20* I came to Meeting this morning to work through my ego and egotism to a feeling of desire to serve. It has happened! Can the Society of Friends help all people do that?

  This does not mean that I wish for an end to all our problems, but rather for the grace to <u>transform</u> them. All through history there have been people and times that turned sorrow into joy, darkness into light. And I've kept thinking this morning of the words of St. Francis of Assisi: "Lord, make me an instrument of Thy peace; where there is hatred, let me sow love; where there is injury, pardon; where there is doubt, faith; where there is despair, hope; where there is darkness, light; and where there is sadness, joy."

Quaker Meeting: A Risky Business

- *Woman, 51** Recently, on Mount Cadillac in Maine, the easternmost point of the USA, I took a photograph of the sun rising, because it was so beautiful. But when I got the picture back, all it showed was a windowframe and my flashbulb reflected against the glass. But I knew what was out there! However it reminded me of all the death and sadness there is in the world. And then I remembered as a child in Hawaii on Easter climbing in the dark up a long mountain trail to see the sun rise—and I was filled with joy.

- *Woman, 55* As I watch a sunrise, I suddenly realize that I stand on an object, the Earth, and it turns! Just before the sun appears, there is a small point of color; it extends sideways; it gets pinker and pinker, a creeping color, a process, and I know I am on a moving body! And when the actual sun appears, the pink then glows all behind me. So I must move into the newness, and this can be upsetting, because I realize that there is no such thing as <u>eternal</u>, time is not endless, time is but an expansion. And so we can know goodness, but we must be renewed, and this can be fearful, too.

- *Man, 73* At Easter I think of the two followers of Jesus on the road to Emmaus, discussing all that had happened, in a mood of despair. And Jesus appeared to them. If I had been advising Jesus I would have told him not to enter Jerusalem but to stay in Galilee, where his words and work were just getting going. I would have said, "Don't go to Jerusalem where people hate you and you will be in danger." But he did enter Jerusalem, knowing what would happen. He was sentenced; the crowds told Pilot to release Rambo (Barrabas) and Jesus was crucified; he was dead on the cross with the guards casting lots for his clothes. From these events a vision and a <u>power</u> were released—and his followers <u>felt</u> his presence on the road, and all things were made new—an act of love, <u>New</u>!—like the sun rising. And we know that love overcomes the world.

- *Woman, 51* On Sanibel Island in Florida there are millions of seashells, some perfect and elaborate, some mere bits, ground by the ocean waters, but they are all beautiful to God; and even the smallest of them changes the shape of the earth.

- *Man, 89* Easter means life, but as I turn it over in my mind, I think of so many who are dead on this earth: like the Arabs destroyed by the chosen people in Israel. And many are dead but don't know it: here in America: the jobless dead, like the robber who broke into our house because of poverty; like the illiterate dead. How terrible, when in America we have a million millionaires. How can all these be raised from the dead? May God fertilize our souls to help do it!

- *Woman, 35* In Luke, Jesus asks, "Why do you seek the living among the dead?" Easter brings new life to us.

---

*This Meeting took place on Easter.

- Woman, 45 My partner didn't want to come to Meeting this morning of Easter. He was born in Czechoslovakia. He remembers that Easter was a day when Christians went out and killed Jews. So: we must face this darkness—and fight against it, not with white gloves and finery.

- Man, 35 Easter is the time for release of power to light the darkness within.

-oOo-

- Woman, 45 This morning I have been asked to read from <u>Faith and Practice</u> the query* on self-discipline, especially as concerns tobacco, alcohol, and drugs:

    Are you temperate in eating and drinking? Are you alert to the dangers involved in the use of alcohol and other drugs?

    Do you refrain from the use of alcohol and tobacco? Or have you considered so doing?

    In all relations with those who have problems with alcohol, tobacco, or drugs, are you careful to be guided by compassion for the individual rather than by a rigidly moralistic attitude?

- Woman, 23 My parents are alcoholics. They are not really married; they are more like "drinking buddies." It makes a very hard life for me, and I am thankful for Meeting where I can escape from the pain and remind myself to love my parents.

- Man, 33 We <u>must</u> love alcoholics. We must be careful not to say, in effect, "I'm going to help you!" Alcoholics are human beings, children of God.

- Man, 37 Really, the only way to help alcoholics is to help them see, <u>themselves</u>, that by themselves they are helpless. And I am amazed that they are able to do this— without any preaching by me. I have found during my eighteen years of working with alcoholics that they are an inspiration to me, because it's not easy to turn your life over to God. They follow the words of the prophet Micah, who speaks words that are very Quakerly**: " What does the Lord require of thee, but to do justly, and to love mercy, and to walk humbly with thy God?"

- Woman, 22 I have been helped by Alcoholics Anonymous, and also by Alanon, which works with families of alcoholics. An alcoholic must admit he is powerless if he (or she) is alone. There are times when all of us must admit that we are

---

*The Queries, as I explained earlier, are a set of questions which Friends ask themselves and ponder the answers. Some are addressed to the Meeting as a whole, some to each individual Friend. In many Meetings they are read at the very beginning of the period of worship for Friends to consider. Through questions, they express a profile of the Quaker way of life and a reminder of the ideals Friends seek to attain.

**Also in Micah are the words, often quoted by Friends "[The Lord] shall judge among many people, and rebuke strong nations afar off; and they shall beat their swords into ploughshares, and their spears into pruninghooks: nations shall not lift up sword against nation, neither shall they learn war any more."

powerless, and yes, walk humbly so that we may be given the power to deal with our problems.

- *Woman, 50* And what about tobacco?—smoke? Our culture is immersed in exhaust, in smoke. If we put an automobile, engine running, in this Meetinghouse, by the end of Meeting many of us would be sick. With so many cars and industries in the world we shall all become part of a sick world. We need to change our culture.

- *Man, 74* Our world <u>is</u> overwhelmed with vast problems. We long for the Spirit. And what is the Spirit? It is the certainty that we can know constant inner love, if we open ourselves to it.

    We should remember Jesus. One could say that he crashed to defeat, and yet from his worldly defeat vast power was released, power that shook the world, that shakes us now. And we must know that love, through us, can empower change.

-oOo-

- *Man, 53* Today we consider the query on Outreach:

    What are you doing as a Meeting to interpret to non-Friends our religious principles and beliefs?

    What are you doing to invite persons not in membership to attend your Meetings for Worship, and how do you encourage continued attendance?

    And to each of us as individuals:

    What are you doing to make others aware of Friends' principles?

    Does your manner of life as a Friend attract others to our Religious Society?

- *Man, 70* Last Wednesday when I was in charge of our one-and-a-half-year old granddaughter Molly, I decided to take her into the Meetinghouse, when nobody was there, just so she could have an idea of what a Quaker place of worship was like. "Does thee want to go?" I asked. "Yes!" she said with a smile.

    So we drove to Meeting, walked in the side door. I held Molly up and she turned on the four light switches, and then we entered this enormous room. We walked around in silence; she explored the benches and the aisles; then we walked up the steps to the facing benches and sat in the place where the closers of Meeting sit on Sunday. We bowed our heads, and I felt a great sense of gratitude for our wonderful house of space and light. Then we went down the steps, around the room again—all in silence—and out the door. As I picked Molly up to let her turn off the light switches, she looked into the big room and said clearly, "Bye-bye," and turned off the lights.

- *Woman, 44* I'm sure Molly had an experience of outreach—a spirit in this Meeting reached out to her. She felt a presence and said, "Bye-bye."

    The other day, in the Social Room [the room just behind the main Meeting room], I was testing a number of candidates for Community Scholarships at Germantown Friends School. The mother of one candidate came along and stayed. She went into the Meetinghouse. After a time I went into the Meetinghouse to see if she was okay. She was sitting in silence. "Shall I turn on the lights?"

I asked. "No," she replied, "I love it just as it is." So, I could see, she felt a presence, too.

- *Woman, 47* You know that our Meeting has given sanctuary to a family of Salvadorean refugees. We who work with them need to feel more strongly your presence as we reach out to help these people.

- *Woman, 42* This place speaks to my condition. I am grateful for the Presence here. I am strengthened.

- *Man, 35* What I feel mainly—and far too often—in my life is the absence of presence. So I come to Meeting for Worship because here I find a presence that meets my needs—each of us finds our own presence, reaching out to us, strengthening us.

- *Man, 75* A few years ago, I was with Ralph Abernathy, the successor to Martin Luther King as head of the Southern Christian Leadership Conference. Ralph Abernathy told me of a time when he knew he was going to be arrested and jailed. Suddenly, a Presence spoke clearly to him: "Don't be afraid. Be arrested; go to jail; don't worry. I shall be there in jail waiting for you."

- *Man, 43* [very much moved] I am in charge of a center for homeless men. We have a new office. It used to be a Cadillac salesroom—a very large room, but extremely crowded—a strong odor of human bodies, jammed in. Off to one side was my office, quite large and unfurnished. Sometimes I went to my office, feeling afraid. I knelt in a corner and prayed and felt I was in a good place—a Presence was there. And so I asked the men, one by one, to come with me into the office, and there I counseled them. And I always felt a Presence reaching out to me.

- *Man, 73* The query we heard at the beginning of Meeting was about outreach to non-Friends. Sometimes, I'll admit, I don't want people to know I'm a Friend. It's because I want to score a point in an argument rather than really to persuade.

    The important thing about this Meetinghouse is for us here in it to ask, "Am I open?" Am I open to the Presence? We cannot really say "Bye-bye," but we must carry the Presence out of the Meetinghouse into the world.

Chapter XI: Conclusion: Always New Beginnings

Just as we must ask, "Am I open?" so I cannot write a conclusion to *Quaker Meeting: A Risky Business*. A marvelous part of the risk is that there are always new beginnings—continuing divine revelation. Meeting for Worship never concludes: we come into Meeting from life; we go out of Meeting into life—often at a higher level; *and* Meeting itself is full of life.

How Some People Come to Join Friends

A wit once said, "Some people are born great, some achieve greatness, and some just grate upon you." Well, there are some people who are "birthright Friends," those whose parents are Friends and ask that their children be enrolled at birth as members; there are some people who gradually, after considerable exposure, become "convinced" and join—called "convinced Friends"; and there are some who suddenly feel they want to join—another sort of convincement. Friends do not use the words "convert" or "converted"—it's convinced.

In the British Quaker publication *The Friend*, August 8, 1988, there was a report on how different people said they discovered Quakerism:

- At age five, I used to cross Liverpool by bus on the way to school. At one bus stop there was a sign "Friends Meeting House." I use to think, "I could do with some friends."
- I thought I was walking into a pub. It looked like a pub. But I found I had walked into a Friends meeting house. I liked it. [The meeting house was Dorchester, and it was a pub before Friends bought it.]
- My little girl saw a notice "Society of Friends" and asked if we could go in.
- I've always had a hatred of organised religion. I am a deputy head in a Church of England primary school. So I talked to the vicar. He helped me to meet the local group of Quakers.

Conclusion: Always New Beginnings

- I was a church cleaner. I enjoyed being alone in there, sitting in the silence. So I joined Friends.
- I went to pick my husband up and went into the meeting house for the coffee. I felt that I had come home.
- I'm very sincere as a person. I found I could no longer sit through the sacraments.
- I was a communist, and I told the Quakers my ideas, and they didn't throw me out.
- My life was saved by the Quaker Center in Berlin. Friends made it possible for me to go to a school in England. Wherever I went to live in England after that, Friends gently sent word ahead of my coming. I was drawn in.
- Quite by chance, someone invited me to come along to Meeting. I was caught.
- The peace testimony got to me.
- I went to an RC school and lived in an Anglican home. I was a natural rebel and incensed by social injustice.

From <u>Zoe Goes to Meeting</u> by David Barlow

What About You?

I know also of some Friends who joined Quakers because of reading about them—in books! I realize that I'm biased, but, since Friends don't go out and proselytize, I would feel it had been worth writing this book if some of my readers, despite the risks and occasional outrages, decided to attend some Meetings for Worship and eventually apply for membership. Reader, it might help make a better you and help *you* make a better world.

But it's a risky business—no guarantees!

Contributors to This Book

I am very grateful to the following people who shared with me for use in *Quaker Meeting: a Risky Business* their experiences in Meetings for Worship. Of course, the list does not include the names of those whose messages in Meeting are quoted, although some of the speakers, coincidentally, are on the list.

Donna Anderton; Margaret Hope Bacon; David Battis; Kathleen Bennett; Frederick Nolde Berger, Arthus Bissell; Derk Bodde; Galia Bodde; Helen Morgan Brooks; Anna Cox Brinton; James Bristol; Carolyn Cooper Brown; John O. Burtt; Samuel D. Caldwell; John Caughy; Polly Caughy; William Cannady, Jr.; Elizabeth S. Cary; Stephen G. Cary; Arthur W. Clark; Mary B. Clark, Marion Cox-Chapman; Heather Cristol; Caroline Davidson; Bunny De Cray; B. J. Elder; Frank Ellis; Francis Emmons; John B. Emerson; Mark F. Emerson; Joseph M. Evans, Jr.; Charles S. Ewing; Ann D. Gordon; Vernon Gotwals; Gladys Gray; Robert Gray; Elmer Goetz; Jennifer Goetz; Peirce Hammond; John Harkins; Marian Hartman; Neil Hartman; Barbara Jones Haskins; Robert Heckert; Bonnie Hosie; Edna Hossfield; K. Ives; Caroline N. Jacob; Mary Hoxie Jones; Rebecca Johnson-Wesiberg; Leonard S. Kenworthy; John H. Kimber; William Koons; Robert B. Kunkel; Lee Laden; Alice Lesnick; Betty Louchheim; David Mallery; Marilyn Booth Manzella; Adelbert Mason; John Massereene-James; Betty McCord; Elizabeth McKie; Carolyn Miller; Cully Miller; Nancy B. Miller; David C. Morgan; Anna S. Morris; S. Francis Nicholson; Louis S. Paulmier; Maguerite C. Paulmier; Ronald N. Pinfield; Jack Powelson; Harrie B. Price III; Eleanor Scattergood Regnery; Patricia Reifsnyder; Jonathan E. Rhoads, Sr.; Harrison Roper; Karl Rugart; Elizabeth McLeod Scattergood; Henry Scattergood; Edmund B. Spaeth; Marjorie J. Spaeth; Joseph Stokes, III; Ann Newlin Thompson; Jeanne V. Vollmer; William N. Waddington; Shirley Waring; Roger Warner; The Rev. Canon Bruce A. Weatherly; Herman Weisberg; Lawrence Stephen Weisberg; Gilbert F. White; John A. Wilkinson; Gretchen Russell Wilson; Margery Wilson; Roger Wilson

INDEX

American Friends Service Committee, 7, 43, 53, 95
Barclay, Robert, 9
Bowles, Herbert, 15, 96
"breaking Meeting," 14
Browning, Robert, 59
Buddha, 35
business, Meetings for, 80-85
Cadbury, Henry Joel, 21, 53-54, 56
Cary, Stephen Grellet, 62, 64-65
Catholics, 73
   on Quakers, 7-8
Chesterson, G.K., 9
children in Meeting, 60-66
Christ, passim
Christmas, 44
Civilian Public Service Corps (CPS), 84-85
committees, 81
conscientious objectors, 84-85
consensus, 81-83
creation, 47
Cushing, Cardinal Richard James, 48
Ellis, Frank, 22
Evans, William Bacon, 9, 52
Faith and Practice, 80-81
First Day, 9
Fox, George, 8, 38-40, 42-43, 80

Friends' Central School, 76
Friends' schools, Meetings in, 67-79
"gathered" Meetings, 94-104
Germantown Friends School, 5 and passim
Glacier National Park, 31
God, passim
guilt, 49
Harvard University, 45
Haverford College, 9, 76-77
Hindus, 35-36
intelligence, varieties of, 28
itching, 98-99
Jesus of Nazareth, passim
Jews, 57-58, 87-88
Jones, Rufus M., 52-53, 62-63
Kenworthy, Leonard, 6
Korean War, 28-29, 96
Markham, Edward, 45
marriage certificates, 93
marriages, 86-89, 93
mazes, 33-34
McLean, Paul, 23
Meetings for business, 80-85
membership in a Meeting, 83-84
memorial services, 90-93
mischief of children, 64-65
money-raising, 82
Monthly Meetings, 80-82
Nixon, Richard Milhous, 8
"openings," 20
Paulmier, Louis, 32-33
Penn, William, 8
Pinfield, Ronald, 22
Pygmies, 35
Quaker Universalist Fellowship, 27
Quarterly Meetings, 80
queries, 48, 102
"rise of meeting," 14
Ross, Betsy, 8
Scattergood, Alfred, 82-83

Index

Scattergood, Henry, 56-57
sense of the Meeting, 81-83
Shiva, 35
slush, 19-20
Swathmore College, 96
Ten Commandments, 46
Tennyson, Alfred T., 25
Theresa, Mother, 38
Theresa of Avila, 12
Vietnam War, 29-30, 95
Warner, George, 16
weddings, 86-89
Whittier, Alfred Greenleaf, 12
William Penn Charter School, 10
Woolman, John, 42
Yarnall, Stanley R., 13
Yearly Meetings, 80-81, 84

About the Author

Eric W. Johnson graduated from Germantown Friends School, Philadelphia, and then from Harvard College, A.B. (magna cum laude, Phi Beta Kappa), and the Harvard Graduate School of Education, M.A. in Teaching. He has taught in independent and public schools, grades five through eleven, and been head of a large Friends' school, Friends' Central.

He is a life-long Quaker. During World War II, as a conscientious objector, he worked with the American Friends Service Committee in Portugal, Morocco, Algeria, Egypt, and India. After the war he worked in Paris (France), Sweden, Moscow, Warsaw, Haiti, and Guatemala. He was involved in famine relief, refugee resettlement, international relations (with diplomats), and international conferences.

Eric Johnson has written or co-authored 51 books, which have sold over 21 million copies. His main subjects are sex education, English and language arts, and humor. (See the front of this book for the titles of some of his works.)

He lives with his wife Gay Gilpin Johnson in Germantown, Philadelphia, and they have three grown children and four grandchildren. He spends most of his time writing books, serving as a volunteer in community organizations, and occasionally consulting with schools and educational organizations.

Johnson lists his greatest pleasures, in *ascending* order of importance, as traveling, reading, jogging, collecting and telling humorous stories, going to Meeting for Worship, arguing, and being married.